The Sedona Table

RECIPES FROM THE TOP RESTAURANTS IN RED ROCK COUNTRY

TEXT BY ERIKA AYN FINCH | PHOTOGRAPHS BY DEBBIE WEINKAUFF

ThreeForks®

Guilford, Connecticut
Helena, Montana
An imprint of The Globe Pequot Press

Text design by Libby Kingsbury
Layout by Melissa Evarts

Library of Congress Cataloging-in-Publication Data
Finch, Erika Ayn.
  The Sedona table : recipes from the top restaurants in Red Rock Country / text by Erika Ayn Finch ; photographs by Debbie Weinkauff.
    p. cm.
  Includes bibliographical references and index.
  ISBN 978-0-7627-4851-8 (alk. paper)
  1. Cookery. 2. Restaurants—Arizona—Sedona. I. Title.
TX714.F563 2009
641.5—dc22
                                                                2008034065

Printed in China

10 9 8 7 6 5 4 3 2 1

Contents

Introduction

Residents of Sedona have a term for the affliction that strikes the four million visitors who flock to our corner of Arizona each year, causing the eager snapping of photos from car windows and gazes filled with delight from those who pull to the side of the road to get closer to the landscape: Red Rock Fever. Truth be told, most of Sedona's residents were struck with this fever at one point or another, which is why 10,000 people now call Sedona home. While it's certainly the majestic red rock formations, with unique names such as Snoopy Rock, Coffee Pot Rock, and Bell Rock, that initially lured us to this part of the state, we stay because Sedona is more than beautiful scenery. Believe it or not, this small town has style.

Sedona, all nineteen square miles of it, sits on the southwestern rim of the enormous Colorado Plateau at a pleasant 4,500-foot elevation. This gives us four mild seasons: Think wildflowers in spring, dramatic thunderstorms in summer, brilliantly colored leaves in fall, and just enough snow in winter to add some drama to the red rocks. Sedona only became incorporated in 1988, but the area's history extends back to 4000 B.C. when hunters and gatherers roamed the land. The Sinagua people lived in northern Arizona between A.D. 900 and 1350, building pueblos and cliff houses and leaving their mark in the form of petroglyphs and pictographs. Ruins and rock art can still be found in the area, most notably at the Honanki, Palatki, and V-V (pronounced *V Bar V*) heritage sites, Montezuma's Castle National Monument, and Tuzigoot State Park. By A.D. 1400 the Sinagua had moved on, but the Yavapai and Apache were taking up residence in the area.

Spanish explorers came looking for gold in the 1500s, staying mostly south of Sedona. Jim Thompson, the first Anglo settler in Red Rock Country, built a homestead in Oak Creek Canyon, just north of Sedona city limits, in 1876. More and more settlers moved to the area to be close to the waters of Oak Creek, liquid gold in the Southwest. And then, in 1899, Theodore Carlton (T. C.) and Sedona Schnebly came to town. The Schneblys located their home where present-day Tlaquepaque Arts and Crafts Village and Los Abrigados Resort and Spa stand; T. C. saw a need for a post office and submitted the names *Oak Creek Crossing* and *Schnebly Station* to the postmaster general. As the story goes, both names were too long for a postage stamp, so T. C. instead chose *Sedona*, after his wife. In 1902 the postmaster approved the name and paved the way for several Sedona Schnebly sculptures located around town, not to mention the bumpy Schnebly Hill Road.

Hollywood discovered Red Rock Country in 1923 when the silent film *The Call of the Canyon,* based on the Zane Grey novel of the same name, was filmed in Oak Creek Canyon near the popular present-day West Fork Trailhead. Since that time scores of movies have been filmed in and around Sedona. The discovery of a ground-water aquifer in West Sedona (then called Grasshopper Flats) in 1951 brought more residents. Famous landmarks began popping up—the Chapel of the Holy Cross was built in 1956, and the shops and galleries of Tlaquepaque Arts and Crafts Village were born in 1971. According to the City of Sedona, the town grew from 2,700 residents in 1970 to 9,000 in 1987.

With that growth, of course, came the need for restaurants, and as Sedona has become more worldly, so has the cuisine. In 1990 the prestigious Chaine des Rotisseurs, the international culinary and enology organization with more than 7,000 members, started a Sedona chapter. The group hosts six dinners and wine tastings each year—look for the Chaine coat of arms, consisting of two crossed turning spits and four larding needles surrounded by the flames of a hearth and the fleur-de-lis, in many of the restaurants in town. In the last five years, some of the best chefs in the state of Arizona have left the hustle and bustle of the Valley (aka Phoenix) for cooler climates and, dare we say it, more sophisticated palates—thus the book you are holding in your hands.

The Sedona Table is the first book to introduce foodies to the wide variety of cuisine and chefs found in Red Rock Country. You will meet fourteen chefs and learn more about their backgrounds and cooking philosophies. Each chef also offers up tips for the home cook, whether it's how to prepare the perfect buffalo steak or the essential tool that should be in every baker's kitchen. You will also learn about twelve different restaurants, ranging from high-desert cuisine to New Orleans–Sedona fusion to classic Italian, and, when applicable, the restaurant's corresponding resort and spa. After years of living in Sedona, we've uncovered an interesting trend: Some of the best places to nosh are attached to some of the best places to rest your head. Each chapter also gives you the lowdown on the restaurant's wine list—13,000 bottles at L'Auberge Restaurant on Oak Creek and 12,000 at Yavapai Restaurant, among others, have garnered the attention of *Wine Spectator* for years now—and includes tips on the best spots for outdoor dining, red rock views, and cozy romance.

Finally, each chef has provided five recipes, including breakfasts, appetizers, dinners, and desserts, many straight from the restaurant's menu. Several of the resorts in Sedona have top-notch spas, and the chefs working at those resorts have labored to create low-calorie menu items recommended by the spa. Three of our chefs have included spa recipes in their chapters.

Love the Sedona Sunrise you tried during breakfast at Adobe Grand Villas? It's in here. Want to impress your friends at your next dinner party with the Pecan-Cumin Crusted Pork Tenderloin with Sarsaparilla Glaze from the Cowboy Club Grille and Spirits, located in the same building that spawned the Cowboy Artists of America? Check out chapter 6. Weren't able to get reservations at the AAA Four-Diamond Gallery on Oak Creek? Turn to chapter 12 for chef Ivan Flowers's Poached Maine Lobster with Seared Diver Scallops, Truffled Petite Brussels Sprouts, and Herbed Lobster Butter.

Aside from catching Red Rock Fever, the visitors who come to Sedona each year are surprised by the variety and quality of restaurants our small town offers—you could stay here for weeks and not dine in the same location twice. Restaurant settings range from urban chic to rustic cowboy. Some locations include live music nightly; and nearly all offer something quintessentially Sedona, whether it's local microbrews, Arizona game (including rattlesnake), or herbs grown in the chef's garden. It was hard choosing only twelve restaurants to include in *The Sedona Table;* do take the time to explore the town's culinary offerings on your own. Still, if you really want to bring home a taste of Sedona, you can't go wrong with any of these recipes. Bon appétit!

About the Cover

Alan McClean has worked as an executive chef in Sedona since 2003. In August 2008 he realized his dream of calling a restaurant his own when he opened Fork in the Road. Unfortunately the restaurant wasn't completed in time for this book, but we're still big admirers of the Scottsdale Culinary Institute graduate. Thus it's his dishes showcased on the cover.

Fork in the Road features European décor, a private dining room, and a communal tapas table with an eclectic, international menu that includes everything from Shepherd's Pie to Prawn Pakoras. "It's about making more out of less," Alan says. "I concentrate on technique and good execution. There's nothing more satisfying than happy customers and nothing better than good nosh and good friends."

Fork in the Road is located at 7000 Highway 179 at the Tequa Festival Marketplace in the Village of Oak Creek. The restaurant is open seven days a week for dinner only. Call 928-284-9322.

1

Jonathan Gelman
and L'Auberge de Sedona

Chef Jonathan Gelman looks at an empty plate much the way those hundreds of painters who call Sedona home look at a blank canvas. Jonathan, executive chef at L'Auberge Restaurant on Oak Creek, uses locally grown, seasonal ingredients in his menu and presents meals in a way that reflects Sedona's artistic reputation.

"Every plate is a piece of art," he says. "Our chefs and sous chefs are extremely talented, and we look at each plate as a painting. We add splashes of color and we make meals unique. We have a very upscale clientele—many are local gallery owners or visitors in town purchasing art—and they appreciate that good food and a beautiful presentation go hand in hand."

Jonathan, always quick with a sly smile and wry comment, studied at the California Culinary Institute in San Francisco. He was the owner and executive chef of Napa Gardens, a prestigious catering company in Northern California, and executive chef at upscale resorts in California and Scottsdale before moving to Sedona in 2006. He immediately went to work at the Four-Diamond L'Auberge de Sedona, a fifty-six-room luxury inn and spa located on eleven lush acres along Oak Creek. Jonathan says he made the move to L'Auberge after years of working for big resorts—the boutique feel of the property was appealing. Of course, L'Auberge's long list of accolades didn't hurt, either. The resort received the Top 100 Readers' Choice Award and was named one of the Top 100 Best Mainland US Hotels by *Condé Nast Traveler*. It has also won the Best of Award of Excellence from *Wine Spectator* for fourteen consecutive years.

A Frenchman built L'Auberge in the early 1980s as eight cottages and a restaurant. The first chef lived in what is today's 2,400-square-foot Creek House, used for executive retreats, bridal parties, and family reunions. The property now includes thirty-five secluded cottages and a twenty-one-room inn with a luxurious great room. Thirty-seven wood-burning fireplaces can be found throughout L'Auberge, making this property a four-season retreat; think feeding ducks by the creek in spring, dipping your toes in the water in summer, photographing the red and gold leaves of autumn, and snuggling next to a fireplace with a glass of red wine and a good book in winter. Ivy-covered trellises lead to pathways connecting the cottages, and trickling waterfalls are nestled throughout the grounds. Large sycamore, Arizona ash, elm, cottonwood, cedar, and maple trees surround the inn, and several grassy areas make it one of Sedona's most popular wedding locations. Joe Mottershead, general manager, says guests, who have included Johnny Depp, John Cusack, and Kurt Russell and Goldie Hawn, describe L'Auberge as a "European lodge with a Four Diamond interior."

"Our guests come here to disconnect at an intimate creekside retreat in the heart of the red rocks," he says. "This is another world from what they inhabit—it's a whole different feeling. Guests who come here appreciate the need to get away from it all."

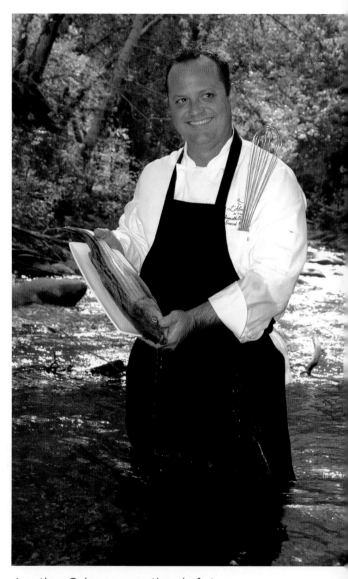

Jonathan Gelman, executive chef at L'Auberge Restaurant on Oak Creek

When Jonathan arrived at L'Auberge, he immediately revamped the French menu—he now refers to the menu as "American cuisine with French inspiration." That French inspiration comes in the form of emulsification and sauces, yet Jonathan insists menu items don't have the "pretentiousness" associated with French restaurants. Pretentiousness in the form of a strict dress code has also fallen by the

L'Auberge Restaurant on Oak Creek

wayside—resort attire works just fine these days. And while he does use imported truffles and oils from France and Italy as well as fish flown in daily from Hawaii (where he was born), Jonathan takes pride in working with local ingredients, including herbs and fruits grown in gardens just steps from the restaurant's entrance. He also enjoys beef and adolescent greens from Tucson, specialty vegetables from the Verde Valley, and lamb from Colorado.

The dinner menu at L'Auberge changes nightly, while the breakfast and lunch menus change seasonally. Popular dinner entrees include the six-course tasting menu paired with wines from the restaurant's 750-label wine menu—wine aficionados can make arrangements in advance to tour the wine cellar, which holds 13,000 bottles. For breakfast, Jonathan says guests rave about the Apricot Brioche Cristo, a house-made brioche stuffed with prosciutto and served with blueberry compote and Chantilly cream. The Shrimp and Crab Louie Salad, a wedge of limestone butter lettuce full of Dungeness crab salad with bay shrimp and pickled red onions, is a favorite item on the lunch menu.

L'Auberge also offers Sunday brunch, popular with Sedona locals as well as hotel guests. If you're visiting during the warmer months, dining alfresco at L'Auberge's creekside terrace is a particular treat (the inn also offers creekside spa treatments, weather permitting). For a really special brunch, settle in at tables underneath trees and so close to Oak Creek you're practically swimming; you'll never want to leave, especially with a wait staff who pour generous and continuous glasses of Champagne.

The glass-fronted dining room is cozy with yellow and green walls, white linen table-cloths, and, of course, a large fireplace, but you'd be hard-pressed to find better fresh-air dining than L'Auberge. Take advantage of it when the weather allows.

Food at L'Auberge is prepared with a deep appreciation for simplicity and health—something Jonathan says he gained while working in Napa Valley, where food, wine, and local farms are part of the town's culture. Jonathan uses fruit extracts for sauces and includes a vegetable and exotic grain—wahine rice, black forbidden rice, and emperor's green rice are his current favorites—with each meal. Lamb is seasoned with salt, pepper, and rosemary, while asparagus is prepared on the grill or salt-roasted.

"Basically, my standard operating procedure is don't mess around with food too much," Jonathan says. "Get items at their peak and don't spend hours pounding, wrapping, and marinating. Fresh food does not need to be overworked, especially if you are utilizing items while they are in season. And don't be afraid to experiment—try something you haven't tried before. After all, it's just food, and recipes are really only guidelines."

Chef Gelman's Tricks of the Trade

"Don't use more than four to five ingredients on a plate, and make sure you balance color and texture—don't use all green foods or all crunchy ingredients. If there is a little bit of white showing on your plate, that's not necessarily a bad thing. Offset the white with a drizzle of sauce. I prefer white plates, but if you are using a colored plate, don't be afraid to use food of the same color—it can still look sophisticated."

At Home

Chef Gelman says he still enjoys cooking for friends and family: "My wife and I cook together every day—it's our only time of the day together." The couple's favorite spring meal includes freshly grilled salmon over salad greens with tomatoes and citrus.

L'Auberge Restaurant on Oak Creek
301 L'Auberge Lane, Sedona
928-282-1667
www.lauberge.com

Apricot Brioche Cristo

Egg Batter
  3 whole eggs
  2 tablespoons milk
  ½ tablespoon ground cinnamon

Blueberry Compote
  3 cups fresh blueberries
  1 cup water
  ½ cup sugar

Brioche
  ¼ cup cream cheese
  ¼ cup apricot jam
  8 slices brioche bread (¼ inch thick)
  4 slices prosciutto
  ¼ pound sliced Swiss cheese
  1 tablespoon powdered sugar, for
    garnish
  ½ cup Chantilly cream, for garnish

1. Preheat the oven to 350 degrees.

2. *For the egg batter:* Place all of the ingredients in a mixing bowl and whisk until well emulsified.

3. *For the blueberry compote:* Place all of the ingredients in a saucepan and cook over low heat, stirring occasionally, until reduced by half.

4. *For the brioche:* Spread cream cheese and apricot jam on each slice of bread. Layer prosciutto and Swiss cheese on one slice. Put both slices together to form a sandwich and dip it into the egg batter. Grill in an ovenproof pan over medium heat until golden brown; flip to the other side and cook for an additional 3 minutes.

5. Place the pan in the preheated oven for 5 minutes or until the center of each sandwich is hot and the cheese is melted. Cut each in half and place on a plate. Sprinkle with powdered sugar. Spoon blueberry compote onto one edge and garnish with Chantilly cream.

Serves 4

Apricot Brioche Cristo

Poached Lobster Salad

4 live Maine lobsters, about 1 pound
  each
1 medium onion, peeled
2–3 cloves garlic, peeled
Juice of 2 lemons
Salt to taste
1 cup extra-virgin olive oil
2 tablespoons fresh thyme
1 fresh bay leaf
1 teaspoon minced garlic
2 sheets brik pastry or 2 sheets phyllo
  dough

Melted butter
2 tablespoons Parmesan cheese
2 tablespoons chopped chives
1 pineapple
1 kiwi
2 tablespoons Champagne vinegar
1/4 cup olive oil
2 tablespoons baby frisée
2 tablespoons baby arugula
2 tablespoons micro basil (petite or
  baby basil can be substituted)
Micro sprouts

1. Preheat the oven to 250 degrees.

2. *For the lobsters:* Remove the tails and claws from the live lobsters. Bring a large pot of water to a boil, adding the onion, peeled garlic cloves, lemon juice, and salt. Drop the lobster claws in and boil for 2 minutes. Add the lobster tails as well, and boil for an additional 4 minutes. Remove all of the lobster pieces and plunge them into a bowl of ice water for 30 seconds to cool.

Chef's Note: If your live lobsters are larger than a pound, they will take longer to cook through; the cooked meat should be solid white, not translucent. You can substitute 1½ to 2 pounds of precooked lobster tails for the meat of the live shellfish.

3. Cut each lobster tail in half with the shell still attached. Pull out the two halves of meat. Crack the lobster claws and remove the meat.

4. In a large bowl, mix the cooked lobster meat, extra-virgin olive oil, thyme, bay leaf, and garlic. Set aside.

5. *For the salad:* Brush one sheet of the brik or phyllo dough with melted butter to coat. Sprinkle with Parmesan, then with chives, then layer the second sheet of dough on top. Slice the dough into 1½-inch strips and wrap each strip around an individual 3¼-inch metal ring mold; you should have eight rings in all. Bake for 8 minutes.

Poached Lobster Salad

Chef's Note: Brik is a thin sheet of pastry similar to phyllo dough; it's a specialty of North African cooking. You can substitute phyllo dough if brik is unavailable.

6. Slice the pineapple paper-thin. You will need three slices per person. Peel the kiwi, then puree it with the vinegar and olive oil. Toss the frisée, arugula, and basil with the kiwi vinaigrette.

7. When the brik dough is ready, let it cool. For each serving carefully remove one circle from its metal ring, leaving you with a circle of pastry. Remove another ring of pastry and place it upright within the first to give the appearance of a basket. Gently stuff the salad mix into the basket configuration.

8. Lay three slices of pineapple onto each plate. Place the lobster over the pineapple and garnish with the dressed greens.

Serves 4

Coriander and Curry Crusted Ahi with Bok Choy, Couscous, Port Wine Syrup, and Soy Butter

1 750 ml bottle port wine
2 cups sugar
4 7-ounce ahi tuna steaks
Pinch of sea salt
Fresh-cracked black pepper to taste
¼ cup (½ stick) unsalted butter, divided
8 pieces baby bok choy

2 cups cooked Israeli couscous
½ cup soy sauce
1 tablespoon fresh-ground coriander
1 tablespoon curry powder
1 pinch micro chives or finely chopped regular chives (top 2 inches only)
1 pinch lemon citrus dust or grated lemon zest (yellow part only)

1. In a medium saucepan, whisk the port together with the sugar. Cook over medium heat, whisking, until the mixture has reduced by three-quarters. Let the syrup cool completely. It will harden as it cooks on the stove but loosen as it cools. You'll need about ¼ cup of syrup for this dish.

2. Season the ahi steaks with sea salt and cracked pepper. In a very hot skillet, sear the steaks for 1 minute; turn over. Cook for another minute and remove from the pan. Keep warm.

3. In a separate saucepan, sauté the bok choy and warm the couscous in 2 tablespoons of the butter until the bok choy is tender.

4. On a warm plate, drizzle some port wine syrup in a semicircular pattern. Slice an ahi steak and fan the slices on the plate at one end of the syrup.

5. In another saucepan, bring the soy sauce to a low simmer and continue cooking until it's reduced by half. Whisk in the remaining 2 tablespoons of butter, then add the coriander and curry powder.

6. Arrange the bok choy and couscous on the opposite end of each plate. Drizzle the ahi with the remaining port wine syrup, top with micro chives, and sprinkle with lemon citrus dust. Finish with a drizzle of soy butter.

Serves 4

Coriander and Curry Crusted Ahi with Bok Choy, Couscous, Port Wine Syrup, and Soy Butter

Colorado Rack of Lamb with Goat Cheese Potato Terrine, Ratatouille, and Lamb Jus

Goat Cheese Potato Terrine
  2 Yukon Gold potatoes
  4 farm-fresh egg yolks
  1 cup (8 ounces) goat cheese
  Fresh-cracked black pepper to taste
  Pinch of sea salt
  ¼ cup heavy cream

Ratatouille
  1 tablespoon minced red onion
  1 tablespoon minced red bell pepper
  1 tablespoon minced gold bell pepper
  1 tablespoon minced purple bell
    pepper
  1 tablespoon minced eggplant
  1 tablespoon minced portobello
    mushroom

  1 tablespoon minced zucchini
  1 tablespoon minced yellow squash
  1 tablespoon minced garlic
  1 tablespoon minced shallot
  1 tablespoon olive oil

Lamb
  2 pounds Colorado rack of lamb
  Sea salt to taste
  Fresh-cracked black pepper to taste
  ¼ cup prepared lamb jus (see Chef's
    Note)
  Pinch of micro sage *or* julienned
    fresh sage
  Pinch of rosemary dust or finely
    chopped fresh rosemary

Chef's Note: You can buy concentrated lamb jus from your butcher; mix with water according to the instructions. You can also substitute homemade jus by cooking beef, veal, or lamb stock with chunks of carrots, onion, and celery until it's reduced by a quarter. Add a bunch of fresh rosemary, reduce by one-eighth, strain, and serve or use in cooking. This jus should be thin in consistency.

1. Preheat the oven to 350 degrees.

2. *For the terrine:* Thinly slice the potatoes. Whisk the egg yolks, goat cheese, cracked pepper, and sea salt together in a large bowl. Slowly add the cream while whisking. In a terrine, layer the potatoes with the egg mixture. Bake for 45 minutes.

3. Season the lamb with sea salt and cracked pepper. In a very hot skillet, cook for 1 minute. Turn over, cook for another minute, and remove from the pan. Place in the oven (still at 350 degrees) for 12 minutes.

4. *For the ratatouille:* In a heavy-bottomed skillet, sauté all of the ingredients.

Colorado Rack of Lamb with Goat Cheese Potato Terrine, Ratatouille, and Lamb Jus

5. Place the potato terrine on a warm plate. Remove the lamb from the oven, place it next to the potato, and add ratatouille. Drizzle with lamb jus, top with micro sage, and sprinkle with rosemary dust.

Serves 4

Grilled Hawaiian Swordfish with Risotto, Brussels Leaves, Watercress Salad, and Almond Caper Vinaigrette

Risotto
- ¼ cup (½ stick) butter
- 1 cup Arborio rice
- ½ cup white wine
- 1¼ cups chicken stock (plus more as needed)
- ¾ cup mascarpone cheese

Swordfish
- 4 6-ounce swordfish steaks
- Sea salt
- Cracked black pepper

Almond Caper Vinaigrette
- ½ cup sliced almonds
- ½ cup capers
- ¼ cup sherry vinegar
- ½ cup olive oil
- 1 bunch Italian parsley
- 2 tablespoons chopped fresh chives

Brussels Leaves
- 1 cup brussels sprouts, quartered
- ¼ cup (½ stick) butter
- ¼ cup shallots
- 2 tablespoons fresh thyme
- 1 cup grated Asiago cheese
- 3 cloves garlic

Watercress Salad
- ¾ cup watercress
- 1 lemon

1. *For the risotto:* In a skillet over medium heat, add the butter and Arborio rice. Cook for 3 minutes. Add the wine and chicken stock. Slowly add more stock as needed. Continue cooking—stirring occasionally but constantly monitoring the consistency—until the rice is al dente. This should take about 20 minutes. Fold in the mascarpone.

2. *For the swordfish:* Season the steaks with salt and pepper and grill for 5 minutes. Turn and finish for another 3 minutes, depending on thickness.

3. *For the vinaigrette:* Mix all of the ingredients in a bowl and set aside.

4. *For the brussels leaves:* Pluck the leaves off the brussels sprouts. Heat a large skillet and melt the butter. Sauté the brussels leaves with the shallots, thyme, Asiago, and garlic until tender.

5. When you're ready to serve, place a spoonful of risotto in the middle of each plate; surround with brussels leaves in a nice design. Place the swordfish onto the risotto. Squeeze the lemon onto the watercress; toss with the Almond Caper Vinaigrette and spoon over one edge of the fish.

Serves 4

Grilled Hawaiian Swordfish with Risotto, Brussels Leaves, Watercress Salad, and Almond Caper Vinaigrette

2

Andrea Carusetta-Blaut
and Sedona Cake Couture

When Andrea Carusetta-Blaut insisted on shipping her baking equipment from Florida to her new home in Sedona in 2004, her husband thought she was crazy. It was hard to fathom that Andrea would come close to her Florida average: ten wedding cakes per week during the busy season. Fast-forward three years: Andrea now bakes *fifteen* cakes a week during high wedding season, in a town with a population of 10,000.

Sedona Cake Couture operates out of Andrea's fully licensed commercial kitchen in the house overlooking Oak Creek she and her husband built and designed. The company officially opened in May 2005, and Andrea's cakes immediately became the talk of the town. She developed a relationship with area resorts and, in June 2007, walked away with three awards from the National Association of Culinary Executives competition in Phoenix, including People's Choice and Best of Show. In spring 2008 she was featured on the Food Network's Cake Challenge, coming in second.

Cooking and baking run in the Carusetta family—Andrea's grandparents emigrated from Italy to North America in the 1920s and opened a restaurant. Andrea herself has been in the kitchen since she was nine years old, baking cookies, tarts, and breads with her aunts and her mom in her home province of Ontario, Canada. At the same time, she was taking private art lessons and would later go on to work in commercial art and advertising until, in 1995 at age forty, she gave up the big income and opened her own bakery, Delicious Desserts, in Dunedin, Florida. Her menu consisted of family recipes and her own concoctions—her absence of professional training allowed her to think outside the box and come up with unique ideas and methods (she even created her own fondant recipe to improve upon the taste and texture of traditional, overly sweet fondant). She says she never intended to bake wedding cakes. Then a longtime customer requested a cake for her daughter's wedding. Andrea agreed, and by 2002 she was baking more wedding cakes than any dessert item on her menu. So she sold her bakery and began making cakes from her home. Her baking philosophy was simple and inherited from her family: Use the purest ingredients and no imitations.

"Most mass-produced desserts use too much sugar to mask the artificial flavors," Andrea says, lounging on the leather couch in the center of her home's great room. "If you use pure flavors, you can cut the sugar back without affecting the recipe—instead you taste the fruit, vanilla, and nuts. Less sugar usually means more flavor."

Andrea puts that concept to work in the twelve varieties of cakes she offers, including Drunken Raspberry Chambord, Chocolate Decadence, and her signature Chocolate Flourless Cake, a rich concoction of dark chocolate that melts in your mouth and begs for a second bite. Her recipes constantly change and evolve—she was inspired to create an Orange Chocolate Grand Marnier Cake after finding a cookbook from the 1920s with a recipe for orange cake in a local antiques shop. She's even managed to create wedding cakes out of her family's delightfully light and airy tiramisu recipe, a typically fragile cake not conducive to layer upon layer.

Andrea Carusetta-Blaut, owner and pastry chef of Sedona Cake Couture

According to Andrea, her Sedona brides—the vast majority of whom live outside Sedona and travel from as far as Paris, New York, and Ireland for their weddings—are less traditional than their Florida counterparts. They incorporate color into their cakes, use different flavors for each tier, and strive to mirror Sedona's natural beauty in a dessert. But it's not just the brides who are inspired by the red rocks. Andrea notes that Sedona has affected not only her wedding cakes but also the desserts she

Sedona Cake Couture

likes to create for her family and friends. Living close to California means fresh fruits often find a way into her recipes, as do the blackberries that grow in her backyard on the banks of Oak Creek and the pomegranates growing on the tree outside her kitchen window. She also likes to incorporate Arizona pistachios—she says she married Florida and Arizona in her Key Lime Pistachio Cake.

An artist at heart, Andrea takes particular pride in presentation. "Presentation is very, very, very important to me," she says. "My primary occupation is food as art; that's ingrained in everything I do. A poached pear on a plate is not enough. I have to add pomegranate seeds and mint leaves." Her signature flourish comes in the form of the edible chocolate leaves she creates using warm chocolate, a paintbrush, and maple, gardenia, lemon, or orange leaves. She swears they are so simple, she taught her mother-in-law how to create one in five seconds.

Andrea's kitchen is also a work of art. Since she works from her home and often has brides visiting, she was determined that her industrial kitchen be as beautiful as her separate home kitchen. Marble countertops, she says, are excellent surfaces for working with chocolate and marzipan. Two six-foot glass-door coolers take up the better part of one wall, with a triple stainless-steel sink under a window overlooking the back terrace. Still, Andrea's favorite piece of equipment is her enormous thirty-quart Hobart mixer. She surveys her surroundings and smiles with the same genuine smile that puts brides from all over the world at ease. "This is truly my dream kitchen."

Andrea still loves baking—her latest venture is painted cakes, on which she hand-paints entire motifs using food coloring. "I am so lucky to have taken the two things I love the most and combined them into one profession," she says. "Every day I feel lucky. I'm always changing my menu and adding new recipes, which keeps things fresh. Each time I meet a new bride, it's a whole new project."

The entrance to Sedona Cake Couture

Andrea's Tricks of the Trade

"When trying out a new recipe, reduce the sugar by one-third, double your extracts, and only use pure extracts. You can even use this one-third rule with pudding and mousse—you will taste more of the cream and butter. And always have a whisk handy; it blends easier than a spoon or spatula. It's the one tool I couldn't live without."

At Home

Andrea loves trying out new cake and dessert recipes on her family and friends—often she incorporates new dessert ideas into her cakes. "My husband does most of the cooking because I bake all day, and we only have dessert about once a week or else I'd weigh 1,000 pounds! My family's favorites include Ginger Crème Brûlée, Molten Chocolate Cake, banana splits, and the truffles I make in the wintertime."

Sedona Cake Couture
928-204-2887
www.sedonacakes.com

Apricot and Grand Marnier Truffle Squares

Apricots
  ³/₄ cup coarsely chopped dried
    apricots
  ¹/₄ cup Grand Marnier liqueur
  5 ounces cream cheese, softened
  2 tablespoons (¹/₄ stick) butter,
    softened
  ¹/₄ cup sugar
  2 tablespoons grated orange zest
  1 egg

Filling
  ¹/₄ cup (¹/₂ stick) unsalted butter
  4 ounces semisweet or bittersweet
    chocolate, chopped

  2 eggs
  ¹/₂ cup sugar
  1 teaspoon pure vanilla extract
  ¹/₂ cup all-purpose flour
  ¹/₂ teaspoon baking powder
  ¹/₄ teaspoon salt

Topping
  1 cup heavy cream
  2 tablespoons (¹/₄ stick) unsalted
    butter
  2 tablespoons sugar
  8 ounces semisweet chocolate
  3 ounces unsweetened chocolate
  2 tablespoons Grand Marnier liqueur

1. *For the apricots:* Place the chopped apricots in a bowl and sprinkle with Grand Marnier. Let stand for 1 hour.

2. Beat together the cream cheese and butter. Add the sugar and orange zest and beat until smooth. Beat in the egg. Stir in the apricot mixture. Set aside.

3. *For the filling:* Grease an 8-inch square baking dish and preheat the oven to 350 degrees.

4. In a small saucepan, melt together the butter and chocolate and stir until smooth. Remove from the heat. In a medium bowl, beat the eggs until foamy and gradually add the sugar. Continue to beat until pale golden and thick. Fold in the chocolate mixture, vanilla, and dry ingredients.

5. Pour three-quarters of the mixture into the prepared baking dish. Spoon the apricot mixture on top. Pour the remaining chocolate mixture over this. With a skewer

Apricot and Grand Marnier Truffle Squares

or knife, swirl together the apricot and chocolate mixture. Bake for 30 to 40 minutes until lightly browned and firm. Cool completely.

6. *For the topping:* In a small saucepan, heat the cream, butter, and sugar to boiling. Remove from the heat and add the chocolates, stirring to combine. Add the Grand Marnier. Pour the mixture over top of the baked, cooled dessert; refrigerate until the topping is firm. Cut into squares.

Serves 4

Blackberry Prickly Pear Cactus Tarts with Pecan Crusts

Pecan Crust
> 2 cups (8 ounces) pecans, toasted
> 6 tablespoons packed dark brown sugar
> 1/2 teaspoon ground cinnamon
> 1/4 cup (1/2 stick) unsalted butter, melted

Filling
> 8 ounces cream cheese, softened
> 1/4 cup powdered sugar

> 1 teaspoon finely grated lemon rind
> 1/2 teaspoon pure vanilla extract
> 1 teaspoon fresh lemon juice

Topping
> 1 5-ounce jar prickly pear cactus marmalade
> 2 pints fresh blackberries

1. Preheat the oven to 325 degrees.

2. *For the pecan crust:* In a food processor, finely grind the pecans, brown sugar, and cinnamon. Add butter until moist clumps form. Press the pecan mixture on the bottom and sides of four 4-inch tart pans with removable bottoms. Bake until golden brown, then cool completely.

3. *For the filling:* Combine the cream cheese, powdered sugar, lemon rind, vanilla, and lemon juice in a medium bowl. Fill the cooled pecan tart shells and refrigerate until firm.

4. *For the topping:* Microwave the marmalade for a few seconds, until softened. Spread on top of the cream cheese filling. Cover the entire top of each tart with fresh blackberries. Refrigerate.

Makes four 4-inch tarts

Blackberry Prickly Pear Cactus Tarts with Pecan Crusts

Poached Pomegranate Pears with Chocolate Sauce

Pears
- 1 quart pomegranate juice
- 1/4 cup sugar
- 1 teaspoon grated orange zest
- 1 teaspoon grated lemon zest
- 1/4 cup pomegranate liqueur
- 4 firm-ripe Bosc or Bartlett pears

Chocolate Sauce
- 1/2 cup heavy cream
- 1 tablespoon unsalted butter
- 6 ounces good-quality semisweet chocolate
- 2 tablespoons pomegranate liqueur

1. *For the pears:* Place the juice, sugar, zests, and liqueur in a medium saucepan. Bring to a boil. Peel the skins off the pears, but do not core them. Add to the liquid and simmer for approximately 30 minutes or until a skewer penetrates a pear easily. Remove the pears with a slotted spoon. Cool the poaching liquid and then add the pears back to it. Refrigerate overnight or for up to 2 days. Bring to room temperature or warm slightly before serving.

2. *For the chocolate sauce:* In a small saucepan, heat the cream and butter just to boiling. Remove from the heat. Place the chocolate (in small chunks) in a stainless-steel or glass bowl. Pour the cream mixture over the chocolate and let stand for 5 minutes. With a large spoon, stir until completely smooth. Add the liqueur.

3. *To serve:* While the sauce is still warm, pour it onto plates and top with a pear. You can also cool the sauce completely and use to pipe designs (with a pastry bag) onto the pears and plates as desired.

Serves 4

Poached Pomegranate Pears with Chocolate Sauce

Southwest Hummingbird Cake

Cake

- 3 cups all-purpose flour
- 1 cup granulated sugar
- 1 cup packed brown sugar
- 1 teaspoon baking soda
- 1 teaspoon salt
- 1½ teaspoons ground cinnamon
- 3 eggs, well beaten
- 1 cup sunflower oil
- 2 teaspoons pure vanilla extract
- 1 8-ounce can crushed pineapple
- 2 cups chopped bananas
- 1¼ cups chopped pistachios, divided

Frosting

- 3 8-ounce packages cream cheese, softened
- 6 tablespoons (¾ stick) unsalted butter
- 1 teaspoon lemon juice
- 1 teaspoon pure vanilla extract
- 2½ cups powdered sugar

1. Butter and flour three 9-inch round cake pans. Preheat the oven to 350 degrees.

2. *For the cake:* Combine the dry ingredients in a large bowl. Make a well in the center and add the eggs, oil, and vanilla. Stir only to mix. Add the pineapple (with its juice), bananas, and 1 cup of the pistachios. Divide among the three cake pans and bake for 20 to 30 minutes or until a tester comes out clean. Cool for 10 minutes and remove from the pans. Refrigerate until cold.

3. *For the frosting:* Combine the cream cheese and butter in a mixing bowl and beat until smooth. Add the lemon juice and vanilla. Slowly add the powdered sugar and beat until very smooth. Refrigerate for 15 minutes or until firm enough to spread.

4. *Complete the cake:* Spread frosting on each of the three layers. Carefully stack the layers one atop the other. Frost the sides and top and sprinkle the remaining ¼ cup of pistachios on top of the cake. Keep refrigerated until serving time.

Makes one 9-inch, three-layer round cake

Southwest Hummingbird Cake

White and Dark Chocolate Velvet Mousse in Chocolate Cups

Dark Chocolate Mousse
  4 ounces semisweet chocolate
  1 cup heavy cream

White Chocolate Mousse
  5 ounces white chocolate
  1 cup heavy cream

1. Make the mousses separately. For each, melt the chocolate in a double boiler and transfer to a stainless or glass bowl. Set aside to cool.

2. Whip the cream until soft peaks form. Add a quarter of the cream mixture to the chocolate and whisk vigorously until combined. Return the whisked mixture to the whipped cream and whisk until completely smooth. Set the mousses aside at room temperature as you continue your preparations.

Chocolate Cups

  8 ounces dark chocolate (tempered) or chocolate coating
  8 ounces white chocolate (tempered) or white chocolate coating
  4 6-ounce Styrofoam coffee cups
  4 12-inch squares of cellophane

1. Melt the dark and white chocolates separately. Place a Styrofoam cup in the center of a cellophane square. Smooth the cellophane up the sides, scrunching the ends inside the cup. You should have a nicely pleated cellophane covering on each cup. Dip this in the melted chocolate. Gently shake off the excess chocolate. Turn the cup upside down and place it on a cookie sheet. Repeat with the other cups. Place the cups in the refrigerator for 3 to 4 minutes.

2. Now dip the cups one more time in the chocolate to the same depth as the first time. This makes the cups stronger. Refrigerate for 10 minutes.

3. Carefully loosen the scrunched cellophane and pull out the Styrofoam cup. Slowly and carefully loosen the cellophane from the chocolate by lightly pulling the cellophane in toward the center of the cup. If one breaks, just re-melt the chocolate.

4. Fill your chocolate cups with the chocolate mousses as desired. Refrigerate until serving. You can garnish with chocolate leaves (below) if you like.

White and Dark Chocolate Velvet Mousse in Chocolate Cups

Chocolate Leaves

Use your leftover chocolate to make chocolate leaves. Start with clean, nontoxic leaves such as lemon, orange, or gardenia. With a small artist's brush, "paint" the back of the leaf with melted chocolate. Refrigerate for 1 to 2 minutes, then "paint" a second, very thick coat of chocolate over the first one. Try not to get chocolate on the front of the leaf. Refrigerate for 5 minutes. Carefully pull the leaf from the chocolate. Use to decorate your chocolate cups, adding fresh berries.

Serves 4

3

Daryl Richards and
The Grille at ShadowRock

Daryl Richards, executive chef at Hilton Sedona Resort and Spa's The Grille at ShadowRock, says that diners who sit down in the southwestern restaurant's high-backed chairs and romantic booths are willing to be adventurous—but they aren't willing to compromise their healthy diets. Perhaps that's why they choose to stay at Hilton Sedona in the first place: The resort puts a high value on adventure and wellness, and Daryl has created a menu reflecting both themes.

"Sedona is a destination where people come to try new things, especially international travelers, which is why our Broiled Elk Chops continue to be so popular," says Daryl, who looks like a young Garth Brooks. "But our number one dish is our Sautéed Shrimp and Scallops because it's prepared lighter. People who come to Sedona golf, hike, and explore—they are more health-conscious. I think we see more travelers rather than tourists."

Daryl has served as executive chef at The Grille at ShadowRock since September 2005. He started cooking at age seventeen when he worked at a restaurant in his hometown of Phoenix. After graduating in 1993 from the Scottsdale Culinary Institute, he worked for several resort restaurants in Phoenix before he and his wife had twin boys and decided to head north in search of a quieter place to raise their children. The 219-room Hilton Sedona Resort and Spa turned out to be the perfect match. It was built in 1998 as the Doubletree Sedona Resort. Hilton, the oldest branded hotel company in the world, purchased Doubletree in 1999, and Doubletree Sedona Resort became Hilton Sedona Resort and Spa in 2001. That same year the hotel purchased the adjacent Ridge Spa and Racquet Club, adding a 20,000-square-foot spa and gym to the property's long list of amenities, which include 14,000 square feet of indoor meeting space (the largest amount of meeting space in northern Arizona), three pools, an eighteen-hole championship golf course on site at the Sedona Golf Resort, and a director of adventure who arranges activities for guests that include jeep tours, white-water rafting trips at the Grand Canyon, and cowboy cookouts.

Since its inception the resort has had southwestern and Native American decor. Drive up to the adobe-style building and a bronze statue of a Hopi maiden gathering water greets you. Authentic Navajo rugs adorn the walls of the lobby, and each guest room, with views of Courthouse Butte, Bell Rock, Castle Rock, and the golf course, includes a gas fireplace. Doug Libby, Hilton Sedona's director of sales and marketing, says the resort sells out most weekends, with international travelers making up 14 percent of guests.

"We are the world's largest hotel company, but Hilton Sedona isn't a big, sprawling conventional hotel," Doug continues. "Every guest is treated as an individual, and we customize stays based on individual needs. We also have a strong focus on wellness. Thirty percent of our guests visit the spa, and we offer a banquet package that includes spa interlude breaks."

The menu at The Grille at ShadowRock includes healthy items recommended by the spa, such as Cured Pacific Mahimahi and Spicy

Daryl Richards, executive chef at Hilton Sedona Resort and Spa's The Grille at ShadowRock

Pecan Salad, so guests with wellness in mind can stay on track. Daryl says there are typically two to three items on the breakfast, lunch, and dinner menus recommended by the spa. (The Hilton Spa has its own eating area; indulge in this writer's favorite treatment and favorite lunch item, The Full Circle and Grilled Portobello Wrap. You can have it delivered to the spa so you never have to change out of your comfy robe!) Spa menu items are generally low in fat, high in protein, and low in carbohydrates.

The dining room at The Grille at ShadowRock

Daryl says people are surprised when they order spa-recommended entrees and don't receive "rabbit food." When trying to cook healthy at home, he explains that it's not always about choosing reduced-calorie ingredients but rather ingredients that are naturally healthy (think olive oil instead of low-fat vegetable spread).

"The two biggest challenges in the American diet are sugar intake and portion size," says Daryl. "There's no such thing as bad food, but rather bad eating habits."

When Daryl started working at The Grille at ShadowRock, which also has an outdoor patio with a fire pit and views of the golf course, it had recently been reno-vated and the menu overhauled. He added a few of his own recipes and continues to change the menu quarterly. Daryl says seasonality plays a part in menu changes, but experimentation, especially among the restaurant's chefs, remains important. Even when trying new ingredients and techniques, Daryl doesn't want to "get in the way of the food." Presentation is important because people see entrees before tasting the food—but again, he doesn't let presentation get in the way of the ingredients.

"I don't believe in sacrificing what makes sense for what looks pretty," he says. "Presentation should catch the eye, but it shouldn't be distracting. Everything that goes on a plate should be edible."

Daryl uses local produce companies and says the nice part of being a chef in Arizona is the availability of fresh food from places like California. The Grille flies in fresh seafood twice a week. Daryl also likes to take advantage of the proliferation of peppers growing in the Southwest—he uses ten to twelve different types of chilies and peppers, both fresh and dried, in his menu items. Peppers, he notes, have the highest concentration of vitamin C of any fruit or vegetable, including oranges—the hotter the pepper, the higher the vitamin concentration. He names the chipotle pepper as his favorite due to its recognizable smokiness. For southwestern cooking he also enjoys working with tomatillos, dried fruits and nuts, and syrup made from the fruit of the prickly pear cactus, which winds up in his elk marinade, vinaigrettes, and, of course, prickly pear margaritas.

The culinary realm is relatively small in Arizona and, just as in Sedona, everyone knows everyone else. But the small-town atmosphere adds its own flavor to Sedona cuisine. "It's a niche market," Daryl says. "There isn't a lot of copying or crossover or unnecessary fusion. Chefs in Sedona do what they do—it's very straightforward."

Chef Richards's Tricks of the Trade

"When you're grilling corn, which is used a lot in southwestern cuisine, leave the corn in the husk because it will dry out if you place it directly on the grill. Also, try experimenting with quinoa, a grain from South America. It's the only grain that's a full protein, and it makes a great grain salad. Cook green chilies in the water with your grain to add some flavor. And if you really want to impress your guests while you flambé a dessert, throw some powdered cinnamon into the flame. It sends off sparks for a dramatic effect. Call it culinary pyrotechnics."

At Home

Chef Richards likes to cook at home but doesn't have much of a chance these days. "My wife is a good cook. I do have a tradition of making duck every Christmas Eve, though, and my guilty pleasure, my specialty, is turkey tacos."

The Grille at ShadowRock at Hilton Sedona Resort and Spa
90 Ridge Trail Drive, Sedona
928-284-4040
www.hiltonsedona.com

Spicy Pecan and Brie Stuffed French Toast with Orange-Scented Prickly Pear Syrup

Batter
- 8 eggs, whipped
- 1/2 cup heavy cream
- 1/4 cup orange juice
- 1 teaspoon ground cinnamon

- 1 cup pecans
- 1 pound Brie cheese, rind removed
- Juice of 1 orange
- Salt to taste
- 12 slices sourdough or oat bread

Stuffing
- 2 tablespoons (1/4 stick) unsalted butter
- 1/4 teaspoon ground cayenne pepper
- 1 teaspoon mild chili powder

Syrup
- 1 cup prickly pear syrup
- 1 cup maple syrup
- Grated zest of 1 orange

1. *For the batter:* Combine the batter ingredients in a large bowl.

2. *For the stuffing:* In a small sauté pan, melt the butter over low to medium heat. Swirl in the cayenne and chili powder. Add the pecans and lightly toast for 2 minutes. Cool.

3. Combine the Brie, toasted pecans, orange juice, and a small amount of salt in a food processor. Blend until the ingredients just come to a paste. Spread approximately 3 ounces (1/3 cup) between two pieces of bread. Dip each sandwich into the batter and pan-fry in a skillet over medium heat for 3 to 4 minutes on each side. Keep warm.

4. *For the syrup:* Combine all of the ingredients in a small pan. Bring to a boil and quickly remove from the heat. Let the syrup cool slightly, then serve it with the French toast.

Serves 6

Spicy Pecan and Brie Stuffed French Toast with Orange-Scented Prickly Pear Syrup

Acorn Squash and Coriander Bisque with Orange Cayenne Crème Fraîche and Pepitas

Acorn Squash and Coriander Bisque with Orange Cayenne Crème Fraîche and Pepitas

Acorn Squash and Coriander Bisque
  6 acorn squash, halved and seeded
  1 tablespoon whole coriander seeds
  1 large onion, cut in medium dice
  3 medium carrots, peeled and
    chopped in medium dice
  1 teaspoon minced fresh ginger
  1½ cups dark or olo roso sherry
  1 cup packed brown sugar
  2 cups fresh orange juice
  Salt to taste
  2 quarts chicken stock

  2 tablespoons fresh lemon juice

Crème Fraîche
  ¼ cup orange juice
  Grated zest of ½ orange
  ½ teaspoon ground cayenne pepper
  1 cup crème fraîche or Mexican
    crema
  3 sprigs cilantro, chopped

  ½ cup toasted pepitas
  Drizzle of pumpkin seed oil

1. Preheat the oven to 350 degrees.

2. *For the bisque:* Lightly oil the squash and roast it, flesh down, on a sheet pan for 25 minutes. Let it cool. Scrape the flesh from the squash with a spoon, discarding the skin. Set the meat aside.

3. Quickly toast the coriander seeds in a small sauté pan until they brown slightly. Cool the seeds, then crush them by rolling them under a sauté pan for 1 minute.

4. In a heavy-bottomed pot over medium-high heat, sweat the onions and carrots. Add the ginger and coriander and stir. Add the sherry, brown sugar, and orange juice. Simmer until reduced by half and season with salt. Add the chicken stock and reserved squash flesh. Bring to a boil, reduce the heat to low, and let the mixture simmer for 60 minutes until the liquid is reduced by a third. Add the lemon juice. Finely puree the soup until it's smooth. Season as needed.

5. *For the crème fraîche:* Combine the orange juice, orange zest, and cayenne in a small pan. Bring to a boil and boil for 30 seconds. Let this mixture cool, then fold it into the crème fraîche along with the cilantro. Garnish the soup with the crème fraîche, toasted pepitas, and a drizzle of pumpkin seed oil.

Serves 6

Dungeness Crab with Yucca Root and Lime Cabrales Emulsion

Crab Mixture
- 1 pound Dungeness crabmeat
- 1/4 teaspoon finely chopped garlic
- Juice of 1 lemon
- 1/2 teaspoon Cholula Hot Sauce
- 1 tablespoon extra-virgin olive oil
- 2 tablespoons finely chopped fresh cilantro
- Salt and pepper to taste

Lime Cabrales Emulsion
- 1/2 cup Cabrales (a Spanish blue cheese)
- 3/8 cup fresh lime juice
- 1/4 cup extra-virgin olive oil
- 3 tablespoons honey
- Pinch of cayenne

Yucca Root
- 2 yucca roots, peeled
- Salt and pepper to taste
- Extra-virgin olive oil, as needed

1. *For the crab mixture:* Sort the crabmeat and remove any shells. Gently squeeze the meat to remove excess liquid. In a small pan, gently warm it with the remaining ingredients.

2. *For the yucca root:* Grate the yucca roots on a box grater using the largest size. Toss with salt and pepper. In a flat-bottomed skillet over medium heat, pan-fry 2-tablespoon portions of grated yucca using a small amount of olive oil. Set aside on a paper towel.

3. *For the Lime Cabrales Emulsion:* In a stainless-steel bowl, whisk together all of the ingredients until smooth.

4. To serve, place some grated yucca on each plate, arrange some crab mixture on top of the yucca, and drizzle emulsion on top.

Serves 6

Dungeness Crab with Yucca Root and Lime Cabrales Emulsion

Sage-Grilled Quail with Grilled Chayote and Apple Relish, and Manchego and Roasted Poblano Polenta

Quail

6 fresh sage leaves
2 tablespoons sweet chili sauce
1/4 cup soy sauce
3 tablespoons fresh lime juice
1 teaspoon mild chili powder
12 quail, bone-in

Relish

3 Gala apples
2 large chayote squash
1/4 cup fresh lemon juice
Pinch of ground cayenne pepper
2 tablespoons olive oil
3 green onions, chopped
Salt and pepper to taste

Polenta

2 poblano chilies
1 tablespoon olive oil
1 yellow onion, julienned
2 cloves garlic, peeled and sliced
4 1/2 cups chicken stock
Salt and pepper to taste
1 1/2 cups yellow cornmeal
1/4 cup (1/2 stick) unsalted butter
1 cup grated Spanish Manchego
   cheese

1. *For the quail:* Finely chop the sage and combine it with the chili sauce, soy sauce, lime juice, and chili powder. Toss the quail with the marinade, cover, and refrigerate for 30 minutes. When you're ready to cook, drain off the marinade and place the quail on a hot grill for 4 to 5 minutes per side.

2. *For the relish:* Cut the apples and chayote squash in 1/4-inch slices, excluding the core on each. Toss with lemon, cayenne, and oil. On the hot grill, cook pieces for 2 to 3 minutes each side. Set aside and let the squash and apples cool to room temperature. Cut the grilled pieces into a 1/4-inch dice. Fold in the green onions and season with salt and pepper.

3. *For the polenta:* Preheat the oven to 375 degrees. Toss the poblanos with the olive oil, place them on a sheet pan, and roast for 10 minutes, turning once. Put the chilies in a bowl, wrap tightly, and let cool. Once the poblanos are cool, remove the stem and seeds. Gently peel off the skin. Cut the pepper meat into 1/2-inch pieces.

Sage-Grilled Quail with Grilled Chayote and Apple Relish, and Manchego and Roasted Poblano Polenta

4. In a sauce pot over medium heat, sauté the onion until slightly brown. Add the garlic and diced chilies and sauté for 1 minute. Add the chicken stock and bring to a boil. Season with salt and pepper, reduce the heat, and simmer for 15 minutes. Reduce the heat to low and slowly whisk in the cornmeal. Using a wooden spoon or a high-heat rubber spatula, stir continuously until tender (about 20 minutes). Remove the polenta from the heat and fold in butter and Manchego cheese.

5. Portion the polenta onto plates, topping each with grilled quail and relish.

Serves 6

Ancho Coriander Seared Ahi with Piquillo Lime Quinoa and Jalapeño Tomatillo Marmalade

Ahi
- 4 dried ancho chilies, stemmed and seeded
- ¼ cup whole coriander seeds
- 6 7-ounce portions high-grade ahi tuna

Quinoa
- 2 ears yellow corn, in husk
- 12 cups water
- 2 tablespoons sea salt
- ½ cup quinoa
- 5 shiitake mushrooms, sliced
- Olive oil for cooking

- 6 Spanish piquillo peppers (or substitute roasted red bell peppers)
- 2 tablespoons lemon juice
- 1 tablespoon soy sauce
- 1 clove garlic
- ½ cup extra-virgin olive oil
- 2 green onions, chopped
- 1 red bell pepper, finely diced

Marmalade
- ¼ cup white vinegar
- ½ cup agave syrup
- 1 very thinly sliced jalapeño
- 1 cup very thinly sliced tomatillos

1. Preheat the oven to 350 degrees.

2. *For the ahi:* Roast the chilies for 3 minutes. Meanwhile, in a small sauté pan, heat the coriander seeds for 1 minute or until they become aromatic. Place the chilies and seeds in a blender and puree for 15 to 20 seconds. Roll the ahi in this mixture. In a medium skillet over medium heat, sauté the tuna on all sides to your desired doneness.

3. *For the quinoa:* Roast the corn at 350 degrees for 25 minutes. Let the ears cool, then remove the husks and cut off the kernels.

4. Bring the water to a boil and season with sea salt. Pour in the quinoa and continue to boil. Stir occasionally and cook until tender, about 20 minutes. Drain off the water and let the quinoa cool to room temperature.

5. Briefly sauté the mushrooms in a small amount of olive oil until tender.

6. In a blender, puree the piquillo peppers, lemon juice, soy sauce, garlic, and olive oil.

7. Fold the corn kernels, green onions, red pepper, mushrooms, and pepper puree into the quinoa and season with salt and pepper.

8. *For the marmalade:* In a medium saucepan, bring the vinegar and syrup to a boil. Add the jalapeño and tomatillo. Remove the pan from the heat and let it sit for 20 minutes. Drain vinegar and syrup and discard. Cool jalapeño and tomatillo marmalade.

9. Portion the quinoa onto plates. Slice the ahi against the grain of the fish and arrange slices across the quinoa. Top with a small portion of marmalade.

Serves 6

Ancho Coriander Seared Ahi with Piquillo Lime Quinoa and Jalapeño Tomatillo Marmalade

4

Nathan Schreiber and Storytellers

It's fair to say the ambience at Storytellers steak house inside Cliff Castle Casino is unlike any other restaurant in the Sedona area. The intimate eighty-two-seat dining room resembles a red rock cave, complete with cozy booths in grottoes filled with Native American artifacts. Recessed colored kinetic lights that slowly change colors to give the appearance of an Arizona sunset softly light craggy walls and ceilings, a trickling waterfall at the entrance welcomes guests, and a chef's table sits in front of a gas fireplace.

Chef Nathan Schreiber's background is as unconventional as Storytellers' atmosphere. A Verde Valley native, Chef Nate, as his co-workers call him, worked at an A&W Root Beer stand and a diner in Cottonwood while playing basketball for a Cliff Castle Casino–sponsored team. He was offered a job as a line cook at the casino after its renovations in 2000 and worked his way up the ladder to become executive chef in 2005.

Nate and his sous chef, Joanne Kenney, launched a new menu in January 2008, retaining the restaurant's favorites such as the Applewood Bacon Wrapped Filet (which is as mouthwatering as it sounds), rib-eye steak, and lobster tail while adding a wide range of sauces—béarnaise, chimichurri, port wine demi-glace, burgundy-marinated mushrooms—to top any steak, pork chop, or roast chicken. Everything is made from scratch at Storytellers, including more than eighty varieties of mashed potatoes and the soup du jour. Fresh fish is flown in from all over the world twice a week. Nate says his philosophy for managing Storytellers comes down to two factors: consistency and flavor.

"People come to dine with us from all over the United States so we need to have consistent meals," he says, sitting in the dining room wearing a tan chef's coat and black ball cap. "I have a good palate, so it's easy for me to take apart a dish to figure out what's in it. It's important to me to taste the layers. Salsa shouldn't be just hot—you should taste more than that. Enchilada sauce should start out with a little sweetness and, after a few bites, you should feel heat on your tongue. No flavor should overwhelm another."

Nate says he always envisions what a meal should taste like when he starts preparing ingredients. It's taken practice, but he now knows that some spices, such as oregano and nutmeg, require only a small amount to make a big impact, while basil and granulated garlic need a bit more. "Be wary of adding too much, though," he cautions. "You can always add more. At home I cook with a pile of plastic spoons next to me. I taste after I add each ingredient."

As a northern Arizona native, Nate loves southwestern cuisine, which is obvious in the Storytellers menu. He works with regional ingredients from prickly pear to masa and chile and even agave as a natural sugar substitute. He says achiote and chilies such as poblanos are his favorites because each crop yields a different flavor. And in the twenty-first century, even a steak house needs to offer items for vegetarians

Nathan Schreiber, executive chef at Storytellers at Cliff Castle Casino

and vegans. Though not on the menu, word has gotten out that Nate will personally create vegetarian and vegan entrees for guests after a brief conversation about their likes and dislikes (by reservation only).

Though Storytellers doesn't have a hunting-lodge atmosphere, Nate points out that it's still a steak house, so presentation is simple: Lemons are tied in nets to avoid seeds, and garnishes include wild orchids, rosemary, and parsley. While many guests come to Storytellers as their end destination, the majority are gamers from

The dining room at Storytellers

Cliff Castle Casino, consistently voted Arizona's best casino, owned by the Yavapai-Apache Nation and located 20 miles south of Sedona. The casino opened its doors in May 1995 with 380 machines and underwent a major renovation in 2000. Cliff Castle, perched on top of a hill overlooking the lush and sparsely populated Verde Valley, now includes an eighty-room hotel, a 9,600-square-foot conference center, a twenty-lane bowling alley, a video arcade, live-action blackjack and poker, 570 gaming machines, live entertainment at the Dragonfly Lounge and the 3,500-seat Stargazer Pavilion, and four restaurants (Nate runs Storytellers and The Gallery). Storytellers has been ranked in the top five steak houses in the country by *Native American Casino*.

Nate knows it's not traditional in Arizona to run a fine-dining establishment out of a casino—nor is it traditional for an executive chef to have no formal training. He revels in being unique, however, and he's quick to recognize the contributions of his staff. Though he's made multiple appearances on local television shows and was recently awarded a gold medal at the Chefs of America Foundation Awards Ceremony in Las Vegas, he insists his notoriety comes from his staff and says there is no yelling or screaming in his kitchen. He works closely with his fellow cooks, even conducting wine classes and wine tastings (pairing wines from Storytellers' always-evolving forty-eight-bottle list is one of his favorite pastimes). He laughs and says he makes all his cream soups backward, cooking vegetables first and adding cream last, a trait that drove his predecessors crazy, and admits he adores experimentation, which resulted in his popular Verde Valley Barbecue Sauce.

"I want to separate myself," he says. "I don't want to be traditional. I want Storytellers to have its own recipes, and I want what we do to be different from other restaurants. If everyone wanted the same thing, why would there be so many different restaurants?"

Chef Nate's Tricks of the Trade

"Break the rules—don't be afraid to change a recipe. If you make something and it doesn't taste the way you wanted it to, don't toss out the recipe—modify it. When it comes to steak, grill it first to brown the outside and seal the flavor, but finish cooking it in the oven to retain moisture. And buy decent equipment for your kitchen. More expensive equipment does make a difference. Better equipment equals better food."

At Home

Chef Nate says he enjoys cooking for his wife and two daughters, especially the wild game he hunts in his own backyard, but admits he goes through phases. "I make a lot of full-flavored dishes. Lately I've been cooking a lot of Thai food in my wok. A few months ago I was all about New Mexican food after taking cooking classes in Albuquerque. I do most of the cooking at home, and I'm lucky to have such a supportive wife—I miss a lot of holidays and work long hours."

Storytellers at Cliff Castle Casino
555 Middle Verde Road, Camp Verde
928-567-7900
www.cliffcastlecasino.net

Southwest Corn Cakes

¼ cup (½ stick) unsalted butter
2 tablespoons shortening
½ cup masa harina (Mexican corn
   flour)
8 ounces creamed corn
3 tablespoons chopped green chilies

3 tablespoons cornmeal
¼ cup sugar
3 tablespoons whipping cream
¼ teaspoon baking powder
¼ teaspoon salt
2 tablespoons cold water

1. Preheat the oven to 350 degrees.

2. Place the butter and shortening in the bowl of a mixer and whip until soft. Continue whipping until the mixture is fluffy and creamy. Add the masa harina gradually, mixing thoroughly. Stir in the creamed corn and green chilies.

3. Place the cornmeal, sugar, whipping cream, baking powder, salt, and cold water in a large mixing bowl; mix quickly. Add the butter–masa harina mixture and mix lightly, just until well blended. Pour into a greased 8x8-inch pan. Cover with foil.

4. Place the pan in a larger pan. Pour boiling water into the larger pan until it reaches halfway up the corn cake pan. Bake for 40 to 50 minutes. Check the water level and add more boiling water if it falls below one-quarter of the height of the cake pan. When the corn cake is cooked through, remove it from the pan and let it stand at room temperature for 15 minutes.

Serves 9

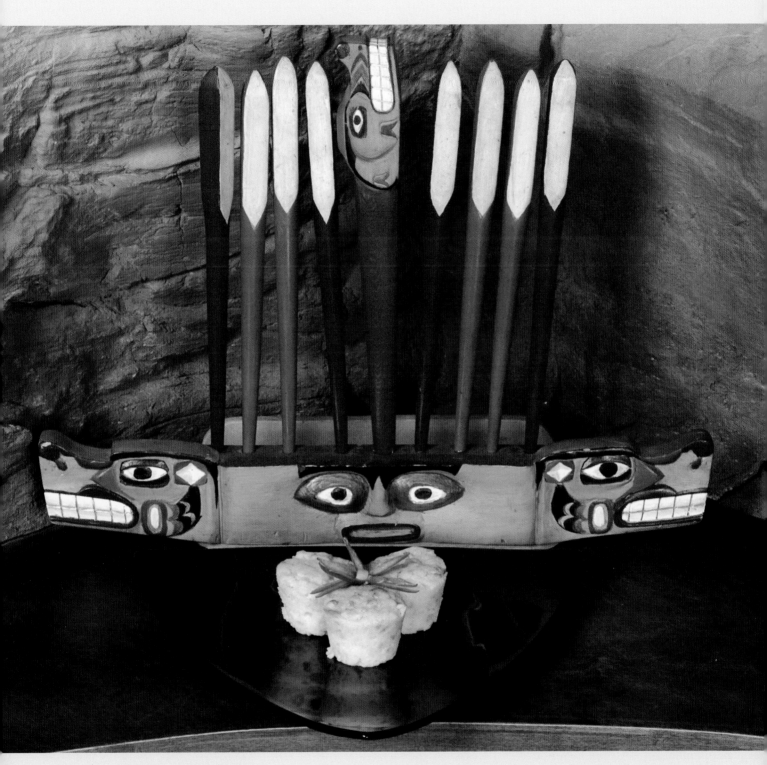

Southwest Corn Cakes

Huachinago a la Veracruzana

1 onion

2 cloves garlic

2 jalapeños

3 pounds red snapper fillets

Salt

2 tablespoons lime juice (plus more as desired)

¼ cup olive oil

2 cups fire-roasted tomatoes

¼ teaspoon dried oregano

12 green olives, halved

2 tablespoons capers

1. Preheat the oven to 375 degrees.

2. Slice the onion thinly. Peel and dice the garlic. Roast, peel, and clean the jalapeños, then cut them into strips. Set them all aside. (It is a good idea to wear gloves or immediately wash your hands with soap after handling jalapeños or any peppers.)

3. Sprinkle the fresh red snapper fillets with salt and drizzle with half of the lime juice, then set them aside in a casserole dish.

4. Heat the oil and fry the onions and garlic, without browning, until they are soft. Add to the pan the tomatoes, oregano, olives, capers, jalapeños, and remaining lime juice and salt to taste. Cook the sauce over medium heat until it is well seasoned and some of the juice evaporates, about 10 minutes.

5. Pour the sauce over the fish. Bake in the preheated oven for about 15 minutes or until done. This is great topped with Cotija cheese and fresh-chopped cilantro.

Serves 4

Huachinago a la Veracruzana

Achiote-Roasted Pork Tenderloin with Verde Potato Chips

Achiote Pork
- $\frac{1}{2}$ cup achiote paste
- 6 cups pineapple juice
- $\frac{1}{2}$ cup lime juice
- $\frac{1}{2}$ cup soy sauce
- 1 tablespoon white pepper
- 2 pounds pork tenderloin
- Oil, for cooking

Verde Potato Chips
- 1 cup buttermilk
- $\frac{1}{4}$ cup black pepper
- $\frac{1}{2}$ teaspoon cayenne pepper
- $\frac{1}{2}$ cup chopped garlic
- $\frac{1}{4}$ cup ground cumin
- Handful of chopped spinach leaves
- Handful of chopped fresh cilantro
- 2 potatoes
- Flour
- Vegetable oil, for frying
- Salt to taste

1. *For the Achiote-Roasted Pork:* Blend the achiote paste in the juices and combine with the soy sauce and pepper. Marinate the pork tenderloin for a minimum of 8 hours. This is necessary to achieve the full flavor of the achiote.

2. Preheat the oven to 350 degrees. Heat a skillet over medium-high heat. Spray or coat the bottom of the skillet with oil and sear the tenderloin on all surfaces until it is browned. Remove the tenderloin and place it on a baking sheet. Bake to your desired temperature, approximately 20 to 25 minutes for medium to medium well.

3. *For the Verde Potato Chips:* Blend together the buttermilk, peppers, garlic, cumin, spinach, and cilantro. Slice the potatoes as thin as you can; cutting them in half lengthwise so they can stack makes a nice presentation. Soak the potatoes in the marinade for 5 minutes then take them out, allowing the excess marinade to drip off. Toss the potatoes in a bowl of flour until they are lightly coated. Be careful not to overdo it or the flavor will be weakened.

4. Add about an inch of vegetable oil to a sauce pot and bring it up to medium-high heat. (Add a drop of water to it; if it pops, it's ready.) Deep-fry the potatoes in small batches—they should cook quickly. Allow them to drain in a colander. Toss them with a pinch of salt while they are still hot, if desired.

Achiote-Roasted Pork Tenderloin with Verde Potato Chips

5. To serve, slice the pork on the bias, let it rest for 2 minutes, then place on plates and serve with Verde Potato Chips.

Serves 4

Café Tequila Grilled New York Steak with Red Rock Ratatouille

Café Tequila Marinade
- 3 cloves garlic
- 1 cup Tequila Café XO
- 1 cup coffee
- $\frac{1}{2}$ cup teriyaki sauce
- $\frac{1}{4}$ cup Worcestershire sauce
- $\frac{1}{2}$ teaspoon kosher salt
- $\frac{1}{2}$ teaspoon ground black pepper
- 4 New York sirloin steaks (or any other steak; elk is also great this way)

Red Rock Ratatouille
- $1\frac{1}{2}$ tablespoons olive oil
- $\frac{3}{4}$ pound red onion, diced small
- 3 cloves garlic, minced
- $\frac{1}{2}$ cup zucchini, quartered and sliced into $\frac{1}{2}$-inch pieces
- $\frac{1}{2}$ cup yellow squash, quartered and sliced into $\frac{1}{2}$-inch pieces
- 1 cup corn
- 1 cup red bell pepper and green bell pepper, sliced $\frac{1}{2}$ inch thick
- 1 jalapeño chile pepper, minced
- $\frac{1}{4}$ tablespoon ground cumin
- $\frac{3}{4}$ cup canned fire-roasted tomatoes
- 2 tablespoons finely minced fresh cilantro
- $\frac{1}{2}$ tablespoon salt, or to taste
- $\frac{1}{2}$ tablespoon black pepper, or to taste

1. *For the steaks:* In a blender, combine all of the marinade ingredients (except the steaks) and process until smooth. Place the New York sirloins in the marinade and refrigerate for at least 4 hours. Grill, basting with marinade, to your desired doneness.

2. *For the ratatouille:* Heat the oil and add all of the ratatouille ingredients except the cilantro, salt, and pepper. Sauté until just soft; add the cilantro, salt, and pepper. Continue cooking for 1 minute more. Remove from the heat and serve with the New York steak.

Serves 4

Café Tequila Grilled New York Steak with Red Rock Ratatouille

Prickly Pear Margarita Crème Brûlée

Prickly Pear Margarita Crème Brûlée

14 egg yolks
1/2 cup sugar
3 3/4 cups heavy cream

3/8 cup prickly pear syrup
3/8 cup tequila
Grated zest of 1 lime

1. Preheat the oven to 350 degrees.

2. Mix the eggs and sugar in a large, heatproof bowl.

3. In a medium saucepan, bring the cream, syrup, tequila, and lime zest to a simmer. Pour the cream mixture through a strainer to remove the zest, and then temper the cream slowly into the egg–sugar mixture.

4. Ladle 6 ounces (about 3/4 cup) of the brûlée mixture into eight appropriate-size oven-safe soup bowls. Place the bowls in a large 2-inch-deep baking pan; fill the pan with hot tap water until it comes halfway up the sides of the brûlées. Bake for 35 to 45 minutes. Remove from the oven when the centers no longer jiggle.

Serves 8

5

Clay Berglund
and El Portal Sedona

Ex-Californians Steve and Connie Segner opened El Portal Sedona in June 2003 with the idea that guests would not feel like they were staying at a hotel but rather a family hacienda circa 1920. Executive chef Clay Berglund carries that philosophy into the kitchen. With only eight people working at the luxury inn, Clay does all the cooking himself, favoring local ingredients—produce from a nearby farmers' market, wine from neighboring Page Springs, olives and olive oil from Queen Creek to the south, goat cheese from Snowflake to the east. All seafood served at El Portal is wild-caught, and meat is certified natural. Clay says he follows the slow-food movement of the Renewing America's Food Traditions (RAFT) organization.

"The slow-food movement is about taste, sustainability, and social justice, such as using smaller, family-owned farms," he says, sitting in front of the river rock fireplace in El Portal's great room and looking out from behind wire-rimmed glasses. "I cook using classical techniques with regional ingredients. With a master's in geography, I understand the importance of sourcing locally from both an environmental and freshness standpoint."

A former employee of the Texas Department of Transportation and a graduate of University of Texas at Austin with a double major in Latin American studies and geography, Clay officially began his culinary career when he attended the Cooking and Hospitality Institute of Chicago, a Le Cordon Bleu affiliate (though he worked as a baker in Austin before his stint with the DOT). He graduated in 2003. While attending culinary school Clay worked at Café le Coq, a French bistro, for two years with chef Steven Chiappetti, a fixture in the Windy City culinary scene. Clay says

Clay Berglund, executive chef at El Portal Sedona

Chiappetti made everything from scratch and became his mentor. "Everything I know I learned in school and from [Chiappetti]."

But not even a mentor can make up for Chicago's brutally cold winters. Clay relocated to Sedona in 2005, doing time at several local restaurants before being named sous chef at El Portal in April 2007 and executive chef three months later. El Portal serves breakfast seven days a week, dinner on Friday and Saturday, and a barbecue buffet on Wednesday (weather permitting); it also hosts special wine dinners. The thirty-five-seat dining room, part of the inn's great room complete with Arts and Crafts furnishings, handmade silverware, and high wood-beamed ceilings, is open to guests and nonguests. While Clay revises the menu seasonally, he says it underwent a major revision and expansion in August 2007.

"My vision is to focus on what the region is all about—and we are a chile region, so I infused the menu with a Southwest feeling with chile as the dominant food theme," says the curly-haired chef. "Chilies have so many unique flavors and tastes— I enjoy using them in traditional sauces such as our elk with a bordelaise sauce infused with dried New Mexican chilies. What people might not realize is not all chilies are spicy, but they add an extra dimension of flavor."

Clay's passion for local, sustainable ingredients mirrors Steve and Connie's own vision for El Portal. The inn is a "green" building, constructed with 18-inch adobe walls and reclaimed lumber, a roof that provides shade in the courtyard and cuts back

The dining room at El Portal Sedona

on energy usage, and Arts and Crafts furniture from Steve and Connie's personal collection. While the inn looks like it dates back to the early twentieth century, it was built in 2003 on one acre of land (virtually hidden from sight but within walking distance of Uptown, Tlaquepaque, and Oak Creek) deeded to Sedona pioneer Frank Owenby in 1901. Guests can dine in the grassy central courtyard surrounded by colorful flowers or simply relax in one of the courtyard's comfortable lounge chairs at the end of the day. All of the twelve rooms, ranging in size from 400 to 800 square feet, are different. Amenities include balconies and patios, whirlpool bathtubs, refrigerators, plush robes, 400-thread-count sheets, and flat-screen TVs. The Governor's Suite has a beautiful adobe corner fireplace, red rock views, a steam shower, and separate sitting area. The entire inn is pet-friendly, one of the first in Sedona.

"El Portal is built like a fine home in Sedona—not a hotel," says Steve. "We

Gated entrance into the courtyard of El Portal Sedona

want guests to feel like we have brought out our best silverware and linens for their visit, yet we are very casual. We sit down and meet with all of our guests at breakfast to help them plan their visit—we have our own tour guides on staff."

Word has gotten around that El Portal is not your average hotel—the *New York Times* and *Arizona Republic* have written feature stories on the property, *National Geographic Adventure* and *Wine Spectator* have both touted El Portal's amenities, and the inn was named one of the eight best hotels in America in 2004 by *Andrew Harper's Hideaway Report*.

"I think we have the best location in Sedona because we are adjacent to the shopping of Tlaquepaque and the fine dining of Los Abrigados Resort and Spa, yet we are not on the street. Our rooms are so nice, many guests opt to stay in, enjoy complimentary wine and hors d'oeuvres in the afternoon, and read books in the courtyard," Steve says. "Guests dine with us when they want a special evening. You can sit and have a conversation with your wife in a room with great ambience and no noise. And we have a great chef."

Chef Berglund's Tricks of the Trade

"Taste everything and taste often. If you buy an apple to cook with, taste it first. Is it tart and does it need more sugar? Is it sweet and does not need anything added? This will help you figure out what goes good together. Cooking is not always about exact measurements and finite rules—that is more true of baking. Vegetables are not cloned, and each one tastes different—you need to know that before you cook. A chef's consistency comes from tasting."

At Home

Chef Berglund says he loves to barbecue and smoke meats such as brisket at home, and he enjoys baking artisan breads on his days off. "When I am at home I like to play," he says. "At work we have the same menu for four months, so at the end of the season I like to go home and play. Some of what I come up with winds up at the restaurant."

El Portal Sedona
95 Portal Lane, Sedona
928-203-9405
www.elportalsedona.com

Birds frequent the feeders in the courtyard of El Portal Sedona

Recipes

Forest Mushroom and Artisan Goat Cheese Quiche

Garnish

- 1 pint cherry tomatoes
- ¼ cup extra-virgin olive oil
- 1 cup plus 2 tablespoons balsamic vinegar
- ¼ cup chopped Italian parsley
- 1 small shallot, minced
- Salt and pepper to taste

Quiche

- 6 Anaheim chilies
- 2 tablespoons vegetable oil
- 8 ounces oyster mushrooms
- Salt and pepper to taste
- 6 large eggs
- 1½ cups heavy cream
- 1 cup (8 ounces) goat cheese

Forest Mushroom and Artisan Goat Cheese Quiche

1. *For the garnish:* Cut the cherry tomatoes lengthwise, toss them in a bowl with the olive oil and 2 tablespoons of the vinegar, and add the parsley, shallot, and salt and pepper to taste. Set aside while you prepare the quiche.

2. Place the remaining vinegar in a nonreactive saucepan and simmer over low heat until it thickens to the consistency of heavy cream.

3. *For the quiche:* Preheat the oven to 350 degrees. Roast the chilies on a gas stovetop or grill until they are charred, place them in an airtight container (a zip-lock bag will work nicely), and set aside.

4. Heat the vegetable oil in a heavy sauté pan until it begins to shimmer. Remove the tough stems from the mushrooms (if any) and place the mushrooms in the pan, making sure not to overcrowd them. Work in batches if necessary. When the mushrooms begin to turn golden brown, salt and pepper lightly, sauté for a few minutes more, remove from the pan, and let them cool.

5. In a mixing bowl, whisk the eggs thoroughly, then mix in the cream gently until just combined. Crumble the goat cheese into the egg mixture and combine. Add the cool mushrooms and salt and pepper to taste.

6. Prepare six 4-ounce ceramic ramekins by spraying the inside with vegetable oil or rubbing with butter. Peel the charred skin off the chilies, then remove the stem and seeds, taking care to keep the chile in one piece. Slice the chilies lengthwise to produce two long strips. Line the sides of each ramekin with the chile strips, being sure to press them firmly against the inside of the ramekin.

7. Ladle the egg mixture into the ramekins. Place them on a baking sheet and bake until just set, about 25 minutes. Remove from the oven and cool slightly.

8. To serve, remove each quiche from its ramekin and place it on a plate. Spoon the marinated tomatoes over the top and drizzle the reduced balsamic vinegar around the plate.

Serves 6

Velvety Mushroom and Oak Creek Apple Soup

12 ounces mushrooms (oyster, shiitake,
   baby portobello)
6 tablespoons olive oil, divided
Salt and pepper to taste
2 large shallots, roughly chopped
2 medium Granny Smith apples,
   peeled, cored, and sliced

¼ cup (½ stick) butter
¼ cup flour
4 cups chicken stock
2 sprigs fresh thyme, stems removed
Chives

1. Remove the tough stems from all of the mushrooms, and use a spoon to clean the gills from the portobello. Cut the mushrooms into quarters. Place half of the olive oil in a heavy sauté pan and heat until it begins to shimmer, then add the mushrooms and cook until golden brown. Lightly salt and pepper and remove from the heat. Reserve some of the mushrooms for garnish.

2. Place the chopped shallots in a soup pot with the remaining oil and cook over medium heat, stirring occasionally, until they turn golden brown. Add the apples and sauté for a few more minutes. Add the butter and, when it has melted, the flour. Increase the heat to medium high and stir constantly for a few minutes, then add the chicken stock. Add the mushrooms and thyme, then bring to a boil and let it boil for 1 minute. Remove from the heat and let it cool.

3. Puree the soup in a blender until smooth, then return it to the pot and reheat. Add salt and pepper to taste.

4. Garnish with the reserved mushrooms and a sprinkle of chopped chives.

Serves 6

Velvety Mushroom and Oak Creek Apple Soup

Natural Pork Loin Filled with Wild Mushrooms

2 pounds boneless pork loin

Salt and pepper to taste

½ cup vegetable oil, divided

8 ounces oyster and shiitake
  mushrooms

1 large shallot, minced

1 tablespoon olive oil

1 sprig fresh thyme, stem removed

1½ pounds red potatoes

2 ancho chilies, stemmed and seeded

1½ cups chicken stock

1 medium butternut squash

¼ cup (½ stick) butter, divided

¼ cup chopped parsley

1. Season the pork loin with salt and pepper, then sear it on all sides in a heavy pan with a small amount of the vegetable oil. Remove from the heat and cool in the refrigerator.

2. Clean the mushrooms and sauté in olive oil with half of the shallot. When these are cooked, remove from heat and add the thyme. Place in a food processor and pulse until finely chopped.

3. Cook the potatoes in water until done. Cool and cut into quarters.

4. Soak the chilies in hot water until soft, then puree in a blender. Bring the chicken stock to a boil and add the pureed chilies. Reduce the heat and simmer the mixture until it is reduced to sauce consistency.

5. Cut the squash lengthwise, remove the seeds, rub with a small amount of oil, and bake at 350 degrees until tender. Cool, remove the skin, and cut into a ¼-inch dice.

6. Cut the pork loin into four equal slices and, with a boning knife, open a pocket. Place the mushroom mixture in a pastry bag or a heavy-duty zip-lock bag with the corner cut off and fill each medallion.

7. Season the pork with salt and pepper and sauté in a small amount of oil over medium-high heat until golden brown on both sides.

8. Sauté the potatoes in half of the butter with the rest of the shallot and parsley. Sauté the squash in the rest of the butter. Salt and pepper both to taste.

9. Place a pile of potatoes on each plate, put one pork medallion on top of the potatoes, arrange the squash around the medallion, and sauce with ancho chile reduction.

Serves 4

Natural Pork Loin Filled with Wild Mushrooms

Roast Duck Breast with Duck Leg Crépinette

2 whole ducks *or* 4 duck breasts and
   4 duck legs
2 medium carrots, chopped
2 stalks celery, chopped
1 large yellow onion, cut into large dice
2 sprigs fresh thyme
1 bay leaf
2 cloves garlic
½ tablespoon chopped parsley
1 tablespoon brandy
2 tablespoons finely chopped truffle
   peelings (see Chef's note)

3 ounces foie gras (see Chef's note)
Salt and pepper to taste
8 ounces caul fat (see Chef's Note)
½ cup blood orange juice
½ cup red wine vinegar
2 cups duck stock
1 cup wild rice medley
2 cups vegetable stock or water
½ cup tart dried cherries
1 tablespoon oil
1 tablespoon butter

Chef's Note: A small amount of truffle oil can be used if truffle peelings are not available. You can substitute duck or pork fat for the foie gras if necessary. Caul fat should be available at quality butcher shops or by special order in the meat department at your grocer; if not, substitute buttered parchment paper and bake in the oven.

1. If you are using whole ducks, remove the breasts, trim the excess skin, and score the skin, taking care not to cut into the meat. Remove the legs, trim out all of the meat, and set aside. Roast the duck bones, including the leg bones, in a 425-degree oven until golden brown, then remove them and let them cool. If you are using breasts and legs, proceed as above, roasting only the leg and thigh bones.

2. Combine the cooled roasted bones with the carrots, celery, onion, thyme, bay leaf, and garlic in a soup pot. Cover with water, bring to a boil, then reduce the heat and simmer for 1 hour, uncovered. Reduce the vegetables by half if you are using only leg bones. Strain and set aside.

3. Grind the leg and thigh meat (or finely chop if no grinder is available) and mix in the parsley, brandy, truffle peelings, foie gras, and salt and pepper to taste. Form into four equal-size rectangles and wrap with the caul fat.

4. Place the blood orange juice in a sauce pot and reduce until syrupy. Add the red wine vinegar and continue to reduce until the mixture becomes syrupy again. Whisk in the cooled duck stock and reduce until the mixture thickens slightly.

  The Sedona Table

Roast Duck Breast with Duck Leg Crépinette

5. Cook the rice in the vegetable stock or water. When it is done, remove the pan from the heat and add the cherries.

6. Season the duck breasts and sear them skin-side down in a pan with the oil until golden brown. Turn and cook to your desired doneness.

7. Sprinkle the crépinettes with melted butter and gently sauté them until cooked through.

8. Thinly slice the breast and fan it out on the plate with the crépinette and rice. Sauce with the blood orange jus.

Serves 4

Mesquite-Grilled Alaskan King Salmon with Leek-Gruyère Tart

1 pound asparagus

6 leeks

2 tablespoons olive oil

Salt and pepper to taste

3 large russet potatoes

½ pound Gruyère cheese

1 bunch fresh watercress

1 tablespoon butter, softened

6 6-ounce salmon fillets

1. Preheat the oven to 350 degrees.

2. Blanch the asparagus in salted water; set aside. Cut and clean the white parts of the leeks and sauté them in the olive oil over medium-low heat until soft; season with salt and pepper and set aside. Peel the potatoes and slice them the thickness of a thick potato chip.

3. Butter a 9x12-inch baking tin and layer half of the potatoes on the bottom. Add, in layers, the leeks, asparagus, and cheese. Top with the remaining potatoes. Cover with foil and bake until the potatoes are tender.

4. Blanch the watercress until tender, place it in a blender with the butter, and puree. Strain and season with salt and pepper.

5. Season fish and grill over mesquite lump charcoal to your desired doneness.

6. Cut the potato tart into twelve equal squares, then cut each square diagonally. Stack the tart on the plate next to the salmon. Garnish with the watercress.

Serves 6

*Mesquite-Grilled Alaskan King Salmon
with Leek-Gruyère Tart*

6

Ty Stuit, Michael Osterman, and the Cowboy Club Grille and Spirits

Chefs and close friends Ty Stuit and Michael Osterman have a history of working together, so it's only fitting that the two are the stars of the Cowboy Club Grille and Spirits, one of Sedona's most popular restaurants, located in a storied building in Uptown. Constructed in 1946 as the Oak Creek Tavern, the building became the birthplace of the Cowboy Artists of America in 1965 (still in existence today) and did time as the town's grocery store. Then, in 1987, California businessman Tom Gilomen purchased the space and several surrounding buildings. Wanting to continue with a western theme, Tom opened the Cowboy Club in 1993.

"I did the best I could to maintain the character of the tavern but also bring it up to code," says Tom. "We kept the original bar top, the fireplace, the barn wood on the walls, and the plywood ceiling. Then we decided to create our own cuisine: high-desert cuisine. It's my belief that you create a memorable experience for people when they go out to dinner, so from day one we've offered buffalo, rattlesnake, and cactus."

Executive chef Michael Osterman joined the Cowboy Club one week after it opened and says developing a menu for cuisine he'd never heard of was a welcome challenge after spending several years working in Northern California wine country and French restaurants. He invented the club's famous Cactus Fries—strips of prickly pear cactus pads sans the needles deep-fried in a tangy batter, a must-have for anyone visiting from outside the Southwest. Michael also notes that the Cowboy Club has become the number two seller of rattlesnake in the United States.

Chef de cuisine Paul Chandler, corporate chef Ty Stuit, and executive chef Michael Osterman of the Cowboy Club Grille and Spirits

"Throughout the years we've come to define high-desert cuisine as foods indigenous to this area," says Michael. "We are a melting pot of cultures: Old West, Native American, and Mexican. For the first few years, as we developed the menu, we had fun experimenting. There was a lot of freedom."

Popular menu items at the Cowboy Club include Chicken and Rattlesnake Tamales, Honeysuckle Crème Brûlée, Prickly Pear Cheesecake, and the club's own flat bread, a take on Navajo fry bread made with cilantro and cumin. The Cowboy Club and, especially, its exclusive Silver Saddle Room and Redstone Cabin at the Cowboy Club are also known for choice cuts of meat including buffalo, elk, venison, wild boar, and a Reserve Steak menu of rare and hard-to-find cuts of beef and buffalo.

The Silver Saddle Room (named after a polished saddle standing inside the doorway) is an intimate dining room located adjacent to the Cowboy Club with tables covered in linens, a cozy fireplace, and a large saguaro cactus skeleton; it opened in 1998. It offers the same menu as the Cowboy Club (except for the children's menu and sandwiches) plus bonuses such as a chef's amusée before each meal. The small Redstone Cabin, located directly behind the Cowboy Club, has served as

The dining room at the Cowboy Club Grille and Spirits

a chiropractor's office, chamber of commerce headquarters, and storage building. With its high-backed leather chairs, art-adorned walls, and courtyard dining, the restaurant opened in 2001 originally for group business. It now serves dinner to the public five nights a week, offering the same menu as the Silver Saddle Room as well as a more refined wine list and wild game specials.

Michael and corporate chef Ty Stuit—easily one of Sedona's youngest top chefs at the age of twenty-eight—met at the Cowboy Club when Ty came on board in 1998. Ty, who grew up in Flagstaff, started in the restaurant industry at fifteen, busing tables at a steak house in nearby Cottonwood. He attended the Scottsdale Culinary Institute and earned the title of executive chef by the time he was twenty-one while working at a resort in Alaska. Both chefs are quick to give credit to the Club's chef de cuisine, Paul Chandler (creator of the ever-popular Bourbon Buffalo Meat Loaf). Paul came on board in 2002 with more than twenty years' experience in Montana, Hawaii, and Oregon. Michael and Ty took a hiatus from Arizona when they moved to Colorado Springs to work at the Marigold Café, a French restaurant, for two years before returning to Arizona in 2006.

"Each time I've returned to Sedona I think I've brought something new," says Ty. "From Alaska I brought seafood knowledge—I know to buy a whole wild salmon

The dining room at the Silver Saddle Room

Ty Stuit, Michael Osterman, and the Cowboy Club Grille and Spirits

The dining room at the Redstone Cabin at Cowboy Club

and cut it myself to guarantee freshness. After working in Colorado I refined my skills and learned about attention to detail and techniques."

Anyone who's visited the Cowboy Club knows that reservations are a must seven days a week. Crowds often spill out the double wooden-and-glass doors, and the wait even at lunchtime can be more than an hour. The back walls of the restaurant are covered with red rock murals, and the entire dining room has the feeling of history—even the salt and pepper shakers are made to look like they just fell off a pioneer's wagon. The bar, with its set of giant steer horns and one novelty seat made out of a horse saddle (a favorite picture spot for many tourists), also gets crowded thanks to specialty drinks like pink Prickly Pear Margaritas (don't go home without sampling one). Michael says it's commonplace to cook for 850 people per day—a challenge in a 400-square-foot kitchen. Tom, who personally reviews all the completed comment cards from his restaurants (an average of 1,000 per week), believes people flock to the Cowboy Club for four reasons.

"We have a great location and everyone loves the cowboy theme—you're never too old to be a cowboy," he says with a smile. "Our cuisine is very unique—tourists get to go home and tell their friends they ate rattlesnake or cactus. And we work very hard to create memories."

Chef Osterman's Tricks of the Trade

"Presentation should be part of the creation process, not just something you do in the end. Pay attention to how you cut the food—use really sharp knives. If you are preparing vegetables, do a trio so you have three different shapes. Score fish skin, properly caramelize meat so it's not burned, make sure there are no lumps in your potatoes, and don't lose your colors when you cook. Really visualize how you want the meal to look before you begin."

Chef Stuit's Tricks of the Trade

"When you are preparing meat, the cooking surface should be as hot as you can get it. And remember to caramelize your meat—it's okay if it turns brown on the outside, you want a nice crust. For steaks it's best to have moisture for flavor, and it's especially important with wild game to keep moisture involved because it's so lean. Buffalo has 80 percent less fat than beef but twice the protein so it dries out rapidly—cook it medium rare or medium. Pair wild game with a sauce or butter to add moisture, or put it in a stew."

At Home

Chef Osterman says he keeps things simple when he's cooking for himself, but he enjoys cooking for family and friends. "When I'm cooking for family, I like to make everything from scratch—even the pasta. I also like to make meat special by pan-searing it and then roasting it on top of herbs, garlic, and onions."

Chef Stuit cooks for himself and his wife on the weekends. "I'm a hunter so I love making fresh quail, but we also enjoy a simple roast chicken. It's about comfort food. I love cooking high-end food, but it's intense, so on my time off it's about comfort food. My dad and I will make raspberry pie together. I'm really just a country boy at heart."

Cowboy Club Grille and Spirits, the Silver Saddle Room,
  and Redstone Cabin at the Cowboy Club
241 North Highway 89A, Sedona
928-282-4200
www.cowboyclub.com

Recipes

Buffalo Brochettes with Peanut Sauce

Marinated Buffalo Skewers

1 12-ounce bottle dark beer (Negra
    Modelo works best)

1 cup salad oil

1 tablespoon chili powder

2 teaspoons salt

1 tablespoon pepper

1 cup orange juice

$\frac{1}{2}$ cup packed brown sugar

$\frac{1}{4}$ cup Worcestershire sauce

$\frac{1}{4}$ cup soy sauce

3 pounds buffalo flank, cleaned and
    skewered

Cilantro Cumin Flat Bread

4 cups flour

$1\frac{1}{2}$ tablespoons baking powder

$1\frac{1}{2}$ tablespoons ground cumin

$1\frac{1}{2}$ teaspoons salt

$\frac{1}{4}$ cup chopped fresh cilantro

3 green onions, chopped

2 cups warm water

$\frac{1}{4}$ cup salad oil

Peanut Butter Sauce

3 tablespoons roasted sesame oil

3 tablespoons honey

1 tablespoon finely chopped fresh
    ginger

$\frac{1}{2}$ jalapeño pepper, finely chopped

$\frac{1}{4}$ cup finely chopped fresh cilantro

1 tablespoon finely chopped chipotle
    chile

$\frac{1}{4}$ cup rice wine vinegar

1 tablespoon chili powder

2 cups creamy peanut butter

$\frac{1}{3}$ cup packed brown sugar

$\frac{1}{2}$ cup tepid water

1. *For the marinated buffalo skewers:* Mix all of the ingredients (except the buffalo) together. Marinate the skewers of meat in this mixture for 12 to 24 hours.

2. *For the flat bread:* In a mixing bowl, combine all of the dry ingredients, including the chopped cilantro and green onions. Using a dough hook, mix on low to medium speed, adding all liquid. Develop the dough for 5 to 8 minutes, or by hand for 10 to 15 minutes, or until it is tender. Remove from the bowl and wrap in plastic wrap. Let the dough rest for 30 minutes. Separate the dough into eight balls and roll out with flour.

3. If you're using a deep fryer, heat oil 2 to 3 inches deep to 350 degrees and fry the flat bread balls for 3 to 4 minutes or until they pop, turning over halfway through the cooking time. Otherwise, barbecue the balls for 5 to 6 minutes or until they pop.

4. *For the sauce:* Put all of the ingredients (except the tepid water) in a food processor. Add the water slowly on pulse mode. Remove the sauce from the food processor and fold it together with a plastic spatula. If the sauce begins to separate, remove it from the processor and add the remaining water by hand using a plastic spatula.

5. *Assembly:* Cook three Buffalo Brochettes per person on the grill. Place a spoonful of peanut sauce on each plate. Cut one piece of flat bread per person in half and place it next to the peanut sauce. Sandwich the cooked brochettes into the bread.

Serves 6

Buffalo Brochettes with Peanut Sauce

Bourbon Buffalo Meat Loaf with Raspberry Plum Barbecue Sauce and Roasted Onions

Buffalo

1 tablespoon oil

3 red peppers, finely diced

1½ red onions, finely diced

2 stalks celery, finely diced

1 tablespoon minced garlic

1 cup Jim Beam bourbon

½ cup molasses

5 eggs

1 tablespoon steak seasoning

6 pounds ground buffalo

2 cups panko (Japanese bread crumbs)

Roasted Onions

1 tablespoon oil

1 tablespoon butter

2 onions, julienned

Raspberry Plum Barbecue Sauce

2 16-ounce cans purple plums

1 16-ounce can diced tomatoes

¼ cup raspberry vinegar

1 12-ounce bottle nut brown ale

4 cups ketchup

2 tablespoons roasted onions

¼ cup orange juice concentrate

2 tablespoons red hot sauce

2 tablespoons molasses

1 tablespoon Worcestershire sauce

1 teaspoon Liquid Smoke

1 tablespoon Dijon mustard

1 teaspoon granulated garlic

1 cup water

Dash of ground cloves

1 chipotle chile

1 tablespoon cornstarch

1 cup packed brown sugar

1. Preheat the oven to 350 degrees.

2. *For the buffalo:* Heat the oil over medium-high heat. Add all of the vegetables and garlic and sweat for 2 minutes. Add the bourbon and molasses and cook until the mixture is reduced by half. Remove from the heat and cool down.

3. In a large mixing bowl, add the eggs, steak seasoning, vegetable mixture, and ground buffalo; mix well. Add the panko and mix well again. Spray a 5x18-inch loaf pan with nonstick coating. Add the meat loaf mixture. Cover with aluminum foil and bake at 350 degrees for 1 hour; uncover and bake for an additional 50 minutes.

Bourbon Buffalo Meat Loaf with Raspberry Plum Barbecue Sauce and Roasted Onions

4. *For the roasted onions:* In a medium sauté pan, heat the oil and butter over medium-high heat. Add the onions and stir periodically until the natural sugar in the onions caramelizes. They should be just brown.

5. *For the barbecue sauce:* In a medium saucepan, combine all of the ingredients. Puree with a handheld food processor. Heat the sauce over a medium flame until it's hot, then spoon it over the meat loaf.

Serves 8

Pecan-Cumin Crusted Pork Tenderloin with Sarsaparilla Glaze

Pecan-Cumin Crust
  2 cups pecan pieces
  2 cups panko (Japanese bread crumbs)
  1 cup granulated sugar
  3 tablespoons ground cumin

Sarsaparilla Glaze
  4 12-ounce bottles sarsaparilla or root beer
  1 cup packed brown sugar

Pork
  2 pork tenderloins
  6 tablespoons vegetable oil
  Salt and pepper to taste
  1 cup molasses

1. *For the crust:* Chop or grind the pecan pieces in a food processor until they reach approximately the consistency of coffee grounds. In a large mixing bowl, combine the ground pecans with the remaining ingredients; mix gently until combined. Set aside.

2. *For the glaze:* In a medium saucepan, bring the sarsaparilla and brown sugar to a boil. Reduce the heat to medium and cook the mixture until it's reduced to 1½ cups. Set aside.

3. *For the pork:* Preheat the oven to 400 degrees. Clean the silver skin off the pork. In a medium ovenproof sauté or frying pan, heat the oil until hot. Season the pork loins with salt and pepper. Add to the hot oil and cook for 2 to 3 minutes on each side or until golden brown. Drain the excess oil. Place in the oven for 8 to 10 minutes, then remove and set aside until they're just cool enough to handle. Remove the tenderloins from the pan, roll them in the molasses, then transfer them to the Pecan-Cumin Crust. Press the crust around all sides of the tenderloins. Slice each into four equal pieces, lay them on a plate overlapping slightly, and top with Sarsaparilla Glaze.

Serves 4

Pecan-Cumin Crusted Pork Tenderloin with Sarsaparilla Glaze

Roast Duck Confit and Cowboy Butternut Squash with Prickly Pear Glaze and Blueberry-Apricot Chutney

Duck Confit

1 cup kosher salt

1 cup granulated sugar

1 teaspoon ground cinnamon

2 tablespoons chili powder

6 bay leaves, crushed

½ teaspoon ground mustard

2 tablespoons sassafras bark

6 whole cloves

6 duck legs

8 cups rendered duck fat

Duck Breasts

¼ cup vegetable oil

6 duck breasts

Salt and pepper

6 duck legs confit

Blueberry-Apricot Chutney

½ cup diced yellow onion

2 Granny Smith apples, diced

1 cup diced fresh pineapple

1 mango, diced

¼ cup sun-dried tomatoes

2 Arborio chilies, whole

2 cups granulated sugar

1 cup apple cider vinegar

1 cup apple juice

1 ounce crystallized ginger

½ cup dried apricots

6 tablespoons dried cherries

1 pint fresh blueberries

Cowboy Butternut Squash

1 large butternut squash

¾ cup (1½ sticks) butter, melted

1 cup packed brown sugar

¼ cup brandy

½ cup water

Prickly Pear Glaze

1 cup granulated sugar

1½ cups prickly pear syrup

1 cup rice wine vinegar

¼ cup soy sauce

¾ cup Frank's Red Hot Sauce

¾ cup lime juice

¼ cup chopped green onion

2 tablespoons chopped fresh cilantro

1. *For the Roast Duck Confit:* Mix all of the dry ingredients in a bowl. Lay the duck legs skin-side down on a sheet pan, coat them liberally with the curing salt mixture, cover, and refrigerate for 24 hours.

2. The next day, preheat the oven to 220 degrees. Remove the duck legs from the refrigerator, wipe off any excess salt with a towel, lay them in a baking dish, and

Roast Duck Confit and Cowboy Butternut Squash with Prickly Pear Glaze and Blueberry-Apricot Chutney

cover them with the rendered duck fat. Cover the dish with plastic wrap and then aluminum foil. Bake for 3 to 4 hours or until the meat falls off the bone. Store in the refrigerator until needed.

3. *For the duck breasts:* Preheat the oven to 425 degrees. In a large, ovenproof sauté or braising pan, heat the oil until hot. Season the duck breasts skin-side up with salt and pepper. Place them skin-side down in the hot pan. Sear for 2 minutes. Drain half the oil and then place the pan in the oven for 10 to 12 minutes.

4. In a second pan, put the duck legs confit skin-side down and heat in the 425-degree oven for 8 minutes or until hot. Remove all of the duck pieces from the oven and let them rest for 3 to 4 minutes.

5. *For the chutney:* In a large pot, combine all of the fresh ingredients (except the blueberries) with the sugar, vinegar, and apple juice; bring to a boil. Reduce the heat to medium high and cook for 10 to 20 minutes or until the liquid is light brown. Remove from the heat and stir in dried fruits and blueberries. Refrigerate until needed.

Chef's Note: This chutney will hold in the refrigerator for several weeks, so feel free to make more than you need. Use it anywhere you'd like a savory-sweet taste.

6. *For the squash:* Preheat the oven to 350 degrees. Peel and seed the squash; cut it into large chunks. Combine all of the ingredients in a 6x6-inch casserole dish. Cover with aluminum foil and cook for 1 hour or until tender.

7. *For the glaze:* In a large mixing bowl, whisk together all ingredients. Refrigerate until needed.

Chef's Note: This sauce is versatile enough to use on tuna, chicken, or scallops; with dipping sauces; and more!

8. *Assembly:* Place equal portions of hot roasted butternut squash on each plate. Prop duck leg confit alongside the squash. Slice each duck breast into five pieces and fan it across the confit. Ladle ¼ cup of Prickly Pear Glaze over the duck and top with Blueberry-Apricot Chutney.

Serves 6

Cowboy Club Mesquite Cookie Sundae

Mesquite Chocolate Chip Cookies

2¼ cups mesquite flour

1 teaspoon baking soda

1 teaspoon salt

1 cup (2 sticks) butter, softened

¾ cup granulated sugar

¾ cup packed light brown sugar

1 teaspoon vanilla extract

2 large eggs

1½ teaspoons pureed chipotle pepper
(more if you like things spicy!)

2 cups semisweet chocolate chips

1 cup chopped pecans

Espresso Chocolate Sauce

1 cup semisweet chocolate chips

1 tablespoon Jim Beam bourbon

¼ cup (½ stick) butter

2 shots freshly brewed espresso, hot

¼ cup hot coffee (or as needed)

Caramel Sauce

2 cups pure cane sugar (do not use
beet sugar!)

1 cup water

½ cup heavy cream

6 tablespoons (¾ stick) cold butter,
cubed

1 tablespoon lime juice

Vanilla Bean Whipped Cream

1 cup heavy cream

⅓ cup powdered sugar

1 whole vanilla bean

Vanilla ice cream

1. *For the cookies:* Preheat the oven to 350 degrees. In a medium mixing bowl, combine the flour, baking soda, and salt. In a large mixing bowl, beat together the butter, granulated sugar, brown sugar, and vanilla until creamy. Beat in the eggs one at a time. Stir in the pureed chipotle pepper. Slowly fold in the flour mixture, adding about ¼ cup at a time, allowing it to be absorbed before adding more. Add the chocolate chips and pecans, folding until thoroughly combined. Divide the dough into twelve personal-size cast-iron skillets; bake for 12 to 16 minutes.

2. *For the chocolate sauce:* In a double boiler, heat the chocolate to the melting point. Add the Jim Beam, butter, and espresso. Mix well. If the sauce is thicker than desired, add hot coffee until the consistency is loose enough to drizzle. This sauce will thicken when completely cooled.

3. *For the caramel sauce:* Combine the sugar and water and bring to a boil. Do not stir—the sugar will crystallize.

Chef's Note: A copper sauce pot works best for caramel. If one is not available, you can use a regular medium sauce pot.

4. Boil the mixture until it just turns a golden brown color. Remove from the heat as soon as the color is consistent; add the cream. Reduce the heat to low to medium and stir in the butter. Turn off the heat and add the lime juice.

Chef's Note: Beet sugar will prevent the caramelization process from happening. Do not let the mixture smoke! If it smokes, you will have to start over. You cannot walk away while making this sauce, because the process happens very quickly. Be extremely cautious around the steam that forms when you add the cream.

5. *For the whipped cream:* Place the heavy cream and powdered sugar in a chilled bowl. Split the vanilla bean and scrape its flesh directly into the bowl. Using an electric mixer, beat until stiff peaks form.

6. *Assembly:* Transfer the hot cookie from its cast-iron skillet onto a serving plate. Top with vanilla ice cream, whipped cream, chocolate sauce, caramel sauce, and the remaining pecans.

Makes 12 large cookies

Cowboy Club Mesquite Cookie Sundae

7

Kyle Evans
and the Barking Frog Grille

Though chef Kyle Evans has been in the kitchen since he was six years old and worked at an Italian restaurant when he was only fifteen, he admits he didn't become serious about a career as a chef until he realized food could be a means of fulfilling his dreams of living in beautiful resort towns and skiing as often as humanly possible. The self-proclaimed ski bum was born in California but grew up in Scottsdale and spent time cooking in Vail, Colorado, before heading to Flagstaff to work under his first French chef in 1995. Being a free spirit and eager to refine his palate, Kyle quit his job in Flagstaff, grabbed his two-week vacation payout and his bag of knives, and headed to Napa Valley.

"I knew it was a culinary mecca, and it seemed like a good place to get some experience," he says, sitting near a large fireplace at the Barking Frog Grille and reminiscing with a grin on his face. "I had no job and no apartment—I stayed in my U-Haul. The day before I had to return it, I got a job at the Napa Valley Grille as a catering chef."

After four years in Napa—a time in which he came to understand and respect the relationship between nearby farmers and chefs—he received a scholarship from a mentor and headed to the New England Culinary Institute in Vermont. Thanks to an advanced-placement program, he finished school in six months and moved to the French Alps for eight months to marry his two passions: cooking and skiing. "When I was in school, we had to draw a picture of what we wanted to do when we grew up—I drew me holding a chef's hat in one hand and skis in the other."

Kyle returned to Arizona in 2003 to be with his future wife and came to Red Rock Country in 2005 to open Reds Restaurant at Sedona Rouge Hotel and Spa—his first position as executive chef. Wanting the experience and challenge of operating a bigger restaurant, he helped open the Barking Frog Grille, owned by Tom Gilomen, the same California businessman who owns the Cowboy Club Grille and Spirits, in the summer of 2007. Where does the Grille's whimsical name come from? Tom says the restaurant shares its name with his twin brother's former Park City, Utah, establishment . . . but barking frogs do exist, making their home in Mexico, southeastern Arizona, New Mexico, and northern Texas.

The Barking Frog Grille and its adjacent Reserve Room are located in a large, 8,700-square-foot, Spanish-style building—both feature high-end southwestern menus. The restaurant is divided into four rooms: the Garden Room, the Fireside Room, the Pond (which houses the bar), and the Reserve Room, which served as the previous restaurant's nightclub. The latter includes the Wine Cellar Room, where up to eight people can privately dine surrounded by 1,000 bottles of wine. The Reserve Room has a completely separate menu, and a more up-

Kyle Evans, executive chef at Barking Frog Grille

scale ambience, from the Grille, but Tom says both "reflect the best of the American–Mexican border." Popular items at the Grille include Caramelized Scallops (served with a colorful and divine sweet potato–stuffed green chile), Snapper Vera Cruz, and the Barking Frog Whole Fish served with handmade tortillas. Signature drinks include the El Presidente margarita made with Jose Cuervo Familia Tequila, the Horny Toad margarita made with Patrón Gold Tequila, and the Barking Colada. Guests at the Reserve Room enjoy the customized tasting menu, a la carte items, and the ever-changing, five-course prix fixe menu. The chef's counter in the Reserve Room gives Kyle the opportunity to interact with diners: "I'll ask guests what they want to eat and the most fun comes when they reply, 'I don't care.' It gives me free rein."

Entrance to the Barking Frog Grille

When it came time for creating the southwestern menu for the Barking Frog—a change from the comfort-food-oriented menu Kyle developed for Reds—he drew on experiences growing up in Arizona and traveling around the region. Kyle says his family often hosted foreign exchange students, including a Hispanic family. His aunt, a surfer, would travel to the coast of Mexico and bring home exotic items such as cactus and tropical fruit salsa. The Evans family also spent time at farmers' markets, which cultivated Kyle's appreciation for healthy cooking. The menu at the Barking Frog includes such ingredients as goat cheese made by Kyle's uncle in the nearby mountain town of Strawberry, pecans and corn from Camp Verde, wines from Page Springs, Desert Sweet Shrimp from a farm in Gila Bend to the south, and apples from Oak Creek Canyon.

The Wine Cellar Room located inside the Reserve Room

Entrance to the Reserve Room at the Barking Frog Grille

"Supporting local farms and focusing on sustainability is really important to me, especially since my son was born," he says. "I think we as a culture have forgotten where our food comes from and who grew it. When you buy from a local farmer and shake his hand, it gives you a personal connection with the food."

Kyle passes that personal connection on to restaurant diners. It's not unusual for him to head to the local tomato farm and handpick fruit for his menu. He also tastes everything created in his kitchen and strives to see and touch each plate before it reaches the customer. "The nights when I only have to touch the spoon to my palate without changing anything show me that I've done a good job training the staff."

Chef Evans's Tricks of the Trade

"Cook with confidence. So many home chefs are intimidated by the kitchen—but you should have fun and just go for it. If you cook with love and attention, it's going to come out good—maybe not exactly what you expected, but it will be good. Also, build a foundation of flavors. Don't just throw everything into a pot—take the time to sweat your onions and add your ingredients one at a time. If you are a beginning cook, master the basics first. If you really know how to sauté, grill, and braise, you have endless combinations of recipes."

At Home

Chef Evans says he cooks at home once or twice a week and loves to grill vegetables, fish, and meat. He's also part of a community-supported agriculture group. "Every week we pick up our bag of groceries and it's something different, depending on the season. It's all natural and organic. I think it's important to support and identify local sustainability."

Barking Frog Grille
2620 West Highway 89A, Sedona
928-204-2000
www.barkingfroggrille.com

Black and Blue Salad

Buttermilk Dressing
  2 organic or pasteurized egg yolks
  1/4 cup red wine vinegar
  1 clove garlic
  1 teaspoon minced shallot
  3/4 cup olive oil
  1 1/2 cups buttermilk
  4 ounces Pointe Reyes blue cheese
  Salt and pepper to taste
  3 tablespoons chopped chives

Toasted Pecans
  1 cup pecans
  2 tablespoons olive oil
  1 tablespoon sugar

  1 teaspoon chipotle powder
  Salt and pepper to taste

Blackberry Sauce
  2 pints blackberries
  1/4 cup red wine vinegar
  3 tablespoons sugar
  1/4 cup water

Salad
  2–3 heads Bibb lettuce, washed and
    cleaned
  1 shaved red onion
  Pointe Reyes blue cheese

1. *For the buttermilk dressing:* Combine the yolks, vinegar, garlic, and shallots in a food processor and blend until smooth. Slowly incorporate the oil into the yolk mixture, then add the buttermilk and half of the blue cheese. Season with salt and pepper to taste and fold in the chives. Set in the refrigerator until needed.

2. *For the toasted pecans:* Preheat the oven to 350 degrees. Toss the pecans in the olive oil, then dust with sugar, chipotle, salt, and pepper. Bake until lightly browned, approximately 15 to 20 minutes.

3. *For the blackberry sauce:* Combine the blackberries (reserve a few for garnish), vinegar, sugar, and water in a pan and simmer for 5 minutes. Blend until it's smooth.

4. Assemble the salad with the lettuce, shaved onion, toasted pecans, and crumbled blue cheese. Drizzle the buttermilk dressing over the top and accent with the blackberry sauce. Garnish with the reserved fresh whole blackberries.

Serves 6–8

Black and Blue Salad

Grilled Arizona Sweet Shrimp

Grilled Arizona Sweet Shrimp

¼ cup dried apricots

1 seedless habanero pepper (or more if you dare)

2 cups apple juice

2 2-inch-diameter puff pastry circles, one with its center cut out, leaving a ring

1 egg, beaten

1 chopped leek, rinsed (no dark green)

2 tablespoons (¼ stick) butter

2 tablespoons olive oil

1 pound peeled and de-veined shrimp (see Chef's Note)

1½ teaspoons chopped garlic

1½ teaspoons chopped shallot

Salt and pepper to taste

Chef's Note: Desert Sweet Shrimp works particularly well in this recipe. It's available from www.desertsweetshrimp.com.

1. Preheat the oven to 375 degrees.

2. Combine the apricots, habanero, and apple juice in a medium saucepan. Simmer for 15 minutes, remove from the heat, then blend until smooth and set aside.

3. Place a puff pastry circle on a sheet pan, brush it lightly with the beaten egg, then place the puff pastry ring on top of the circle and press gently to seal. Bake for 10 minutes.

4. Sauté the leeks in the butter until soft and tender.

5. Heat the olive oil in a sauté pan on medium-high heat, add the shrimp, cook for 2 minutes, then add the garlic, shallots, and salt and pepper to taste.

6. To serve, spoon some apricot sauce onto each plate, place the braised leeks in the center of the plate inside the pastry, and arrange the shrimp around each leek-filled pastry.

Serves 6–8

Braised Short Ribs

2 3-pound short ribs, bone-in, 2–3
  inches
3 tablespoons olive oil
1 onion, chopped
1 leek, rinsed well and chopped
1 large carrot, chopped
1 head garlic, split
3 cups red wine (Syrah is
  recommended)

1½ quarts veal stock
3 Oaxaca chilies
1 teaspoon ground cumin seeds
¼ teaspoon ground cardamom
1 teaspoon dried Mexican oregano
1 bay leaf
Fresh thyme sprigs
2 tablespoons tomato paste
1 ounce Mexican chocolate (optional)

1. Preheat the oven to 300 degrees.

2. In a large roasting pan, sauté the short ribs in the olive oil until browned. Add the onion, leek, carrot, and garlic; sauté for several minutes. Deglaze the pan with the red wine. Let the wine reduce by half, then add the veal stock and remaining ingredients (except the chocolate, if you're using it). Let this mixture simmer for a few minutes.

3. Cover the pan with foil and put it in the oven; let it bake for approximately 3 hours until the meat is fork-tender. Remove the short ribs from the stock, then strain the stock and reduce it to your desired consistency. Add the chocolate toward the end, if desired.

Serves 6–8

Braised Short Ribs

Barking Frog Whole Fish

Barking Frog Whole Fish

1 whole fish, 1–2 pounds, cleaned and
   descaled (red snapper works well in
   this recipe)
2 quarts oil
2 cups flour
1 tablespoon New Mexican chili powder

1 tablespoon guajillo chile powder
$\frac{1}{4}$ teaspoon de arbol chile powder
1 tablespoon garlic powder
1 tablespoon paprika
1 teaspoon black pepper
1 tablespoon kosher salt

1. In a deep fryer or large saucepan, heat the oil to 350 degrees.

2. With a razor blade, slice three or four thin slits along the skin on each side of the
fish.

3. Mix all of the dry ingredients in a bowl, then cover the fish with the flour mixture.

4. Gently submerge the dusted fish into the hot oil. Cook for 7 to 10 minutes until
the fish is crispy and cooked through. Serve with traditional condiments such as tortillas, limes, shredded cabbage, and pico de gallo.

Serves 2

Lemon Masa Crepe Brûlée

Masa Crepe
- 1 cup plus 2 tablespoons masa flour
- 1 cup plus 2 tablespoons all-purpose flour
- 1 whole vanilla bean
- 3¼ cups milk
- ½ cup sugar
- 2 eggs
- ⅜ cup beurre noisette (brown butter)
- ¼ cup Grand Marnier liqueur
- 1 cup additional milk (or as needed for thinning the batter)

Lemon Curd
- 6 eggs
- ½ cup lemon juice
- ½ cup sugar
- 1½ cups (3 sticks) butter

1. *For the crepe:* Sift together the masa flour and all-purpose flour. Scrape the seeds from the vanilla bean and place them in a pot with the milk and sugar. Over high heat, bring the mixture just to a boil. Remove from the heat.

2. In a separate bowl, whisk the 2 eggs. Temper in the hot milk. Whisk in the flour mixture. Add the beurre noisette and Grand Marnier. Place the batter into a blender and blend at high speed. (You may need to thin the batter with remaining 1 cup of milk. It should have the consistency of very thin pancake batter.) Strain through a fine-mesh strainer. Refrigerate overnight.

3. *For the lemon curd:* Place the 6 eggs, lemon juice, and sugar in a pot. Heat over a medium flame, whisking constantly. Cut the cold butter into medium chunks. Once the mixture is thick enough to coat the back of a spoon, add the butter one piece at a time while continuing to whisk until the butter is absorbed.

4. Transfer the lemon curd into a container, sprinkling a bit of sugar on top (this will prevent the curd from forming a skin). Wrap tightly with plastic wrap and refrigerate until it sets up.

5. Butter a 10-inch nonstick sauté pan. Place over high heat. Pour 2 ounces of crepe batter into the pan, working in a circular motion until the pan is completely coated with batter. Reduce the heat to low and cook until the crepe turns golden brown. Flip it over onto a clean work surface. Add about 3 tablespoons of lemon curd in the middle of the crepe. Fold in the crepe on the sides to form a square, then carefully flip it over. Brush with melted butter, sprinkle with sugar, and brown the sugar with a torch.

6. Continue making crepes this way with the remaining batter and lemon curd.

Serves 6–8

Lemon Masa Crepe Brûlée

8

Michael Parnell
and the Inn on Oak Creek

At 3:00 a.m., six days a week, Michael Parnell climbs out of bed, careful not to wake his two sleeping sons, and drives from his home in Camp Verde to the Inn on Oak Creek to prepare four-course breakfasts from scratch. He returns home before noon each day to greet his boys when they are finished with school and says he doesn't mind the early hours. With short blond hair and arms covered in tattoos, Michael looks like he'd be at home as a roadie for a rock band, not like a single father who's worked in the food industry for thirteen years. He smiles shyly when asked what keeps him motivated when the predawn alarm clock buzzes.

"I know people enjoy my food—I hear the feedback and it's very gratifying," he says. "I cook for different people every day, and sometimes the guests wander into the kitchen to ask questions or want to have their picture taken with me. It makes it easy to get up early in the morning."

Michael has been at the Four Diamond inn, located on the banks of Oak Creek, since 2006. He started cooking breakfast in his mom's California kitchen; his first job was at a fast-food joint when he was fourteen. After graduating from the Western Culinary Institute in Portland, Oregon, in 2002 he moved to northern Arizona and worked at several prestigious eateries and bakeries before landing at the Inn on Oak Creek. He prepares all meals on his own without any assistance; the inn's owner, Jim Matykiewicz, fills in for Michael on his days off. Michael plans out his breakfasts one week in advance, using only his own recipes, including favorites such as Roasted Jalapeño Corn Bread, Caramelized Bananas with Pecan Rum Butter Sauce, Chocolate Stuffed French Toast with Red Raspberry Sauce, and seasonal fresh fruit smoothies.

Michael Parnell, executive chef at the Inn on Oak Creek

Though Michael attended culinary school, he says there's nothing like "trial by fire." The freedom he enjoys at the inn allows for experimentation, and he's come to understand which flavors work best together. Every morning guests receive a sweet and a savory pastry to appease any diner (though we've yet to meet someone who didn't indulge in both), and he rotates each day between egg dishes and sweet dishes such as pancakes and waffles. Michael also takes pride in getting his hands dirty, literally, as often as possible. While the kitchen at the inn is decked out with the latest and greatest equipment, Michael prefers working with his hands for "more control."

"It's what I was taught at home and at school," he says. "My parents used to tell me I couldn't get paid for playing with my food and now all I do is play with food! But seriously, I think it gives you more experience, and the art of cooking comes to you faster when you see and feel how ingredients react to each other. It might take longer to do it by hand rather than with a machine, but you'll get fast."

Gourmet breakfasts are only part of the food experience at the inn. Jim, who purchased the property in 2005, added a cooking school, the Art of Cooking, in 2007. The Art of Cooking features guest chefs from restaurants and resorts as far away as Phoenix on Tuesday and Thursday evenings. The chef hands out four-course

The Inn on Oak Creek

menus to up to twelve guests, explains techniques, and then enlists the help of everyone to prepare the meal. Would-be gourmets dine together around the kitchen's sixteen-foot island, and guests leave with recipes to prepare for friends and family at home. It's just an extension of the inn's cozy, home-away-from-home feeling.

Built in 1977 as an art gallery, the Inn on Oak Creek was born in 1995 with eleven themed rooms including the Angler's Retreat, Hollywood Out West, Homestead Hearts, and Trading Post. Seven of the rooms have decks overlooking Oak Creek; all are equipped with Jacuzzi tubs and gas fireplaces.

Walk through the inn's copper-and-etched-glass doors and you're in a comfortable great room with a fireplace surrounded by plush floral-print couches, hardwood floors and pine dining tables, and large windows with views of Oak Creek, Wilson Mountain, and the neighboring creekside park at Los Abrigados Resort and Spa. The decor can only be described as Country French with a western flair. Niches are filled with teapots and Navajo kachinas, while paintings of the Grand Canyon and French cafes adorn the walls. Guests can dine indoors but, for a real treat, enjoy breakfast during the warmer months on the deck perched over Oak Creek—the tranquil sound of flowing water beckons diners to lounge until lunchtime. The inn keeps a supply of leftover bread so guests can feed the ducks that congregate below the deck and

Great room at the Inn on Oak Creek

along the banks of the private park. It's not unusual for a huge blue heron to swoop across the creek; javelinas are often spotted as well, though Jim cautions people not to feed or pet the wild peccaries.

Unlike most European B&Bs, dining at the Inn on Oak Creek isn't communal unless you want it to be—all parties receive their own table. Many guests come to breakfast in their pajamas and robes, and hors d'oeuvres are served each evening from 5:00 to 6:00 p.m. (fresh cookies are out twenty-four hours a day). Breakfast at the inn is open to nonguests if there is room (reservations made at least twenty-four hours in advance are required), but it's not highly publicized, making this one of Sedona locals' best-kept breakfast secrets. Michael is also available for private dinner parties at the inn with advance notice.

"We hear from quite a few people that they feel at home with us while at the same time they are getting away from it all," says Jim. "It makes us feel good. We're definitely not a cookie-cutter hotel operation."

Chef Parnell's Tricks of the Trade

"If you're making a sweet dish with chocolate, balance it with tartness such as a fruit coulis. Add lemon juice to butter to keep the butter from sticking to the palate. If you are going for a southwestern flair, garnish your plate with avocado and tomato for southwestern colors. And if you don't have a sharp mind and a sharp knife, then stay out of the kitchen!"

At Home

Ironically, Chef Parnell is not a breakfast person and says he rarely eats before noon, though he does sample everything he creates. His sons, however, love it when Dad makes breakfast. "They will plan the day before what they want to eat, and oftentimes it's chocolate chip pancakes," he says. "Two years ago we drove to California for my great-grandmother's birthday and the first thing she asked me was, 'What's for dinner?' My family loves it when I cook, whether it's breakfast, lunch, or dinner."

The Inn on Oak Creek
556 Highway 179, Sedona
928-282-7896
www.innonoakcreek.com

Recipes

Roasted Jalapeño Corn Bread

1¼ cups all-purpose flour
1¼ cups yellow cornmeal
1¼ teaspoons baking powder
¾ teaspoon salt
1 tablespoon sugar
1 tablespoon garlic salt
1 teaspoon onion powder
1 fresh red bell pepper, roasted and
    finely diced

2 fresh jalapeño peppers, roasted and
    finely diced
¼ cup diced red onion
3 large eggs
1¼ cups whole milk
¾ cup vegetable oil

Preheat the oven to 400 degrees. Lightly grease a 9x13-inch glass baking pan. Combine the dry ingredients in a medium mixing bowl. Mix in the peppers, onion, and wet ingredients. Pour into the prepared baking pan and bake for 20 minutes.

Serves 6

Roasted Jalapeño Corn Bread

Chocolate-Stuffed French Toast on Challah Bread with Red Raspberry Sauce

1 loaf challah bread
12 ounces semisweet chocolate
6 eggs
½ cup whole milk
1 tablespoon ground cinnamon
2 teaspoons pure vanilla extract

Raspberry Sauce
1 pint fresh raspberries
1 tablespoon sugar
2 teaspoons water

1. *For the French toast:* Slice the challah bread into twelve slices. Finely chop the chocolate and set aside. In a medium mixing bowl, add the eggs, milk, cinnamon, and vanilla and beat together. Dip each piece of bread into the egg wash and place in a hot frying pan. Flip over once. Sprinkle chopped chocolate onto one slice of bread and add another slice on top. Cut in half.

2. *For the sauce:* Blend the raspberries in a blender with the sugar and water, then strain through a fine strainer. Pour the sauce on top of the French toast and serve warm.

Serves 6

Chocolate-Stuffed French Toast on Challah Bread with Red Raspberry Sauce

Savory Four-Cheese Strata with Avocado and Tomato

24 eggs
2 cups whole milk
1 teaspoon onion powder
1 tablespoon garlic salt
6 slices white bread
4 ounces shredded Cheddar cheese

4 ounces shredded dill Havarti cheese
4 ounces shredded jalapeño Jack
cheese
4 ounces shredded smoked Gouda
2 whole avocados
2 whole steak tomatoes

1. Preheat the oven to 350 degrees. Thoroughly grease a 9x13-inch glass baking pan.

2. Combine the eggs, milk, onion powder, and garlic salt. Blend together.

3. Crumble the bread and place it in the prepared baking pan. Cover the bread with the cheeses, pour the egg mixture over the top, and bake for 1 hour. Garnish with avocado and tomato.

Serves 6

Savory Four-Cheese Strata with Avocado and Tomato

Chocolate Cream Puffs

Cream Puffs
- 1 cup all-purpose flour
- $^3/_4$ teaspoon baking powder
- $^1/_2$ teaspoon salt
- $^1/_2$ cup (1 stick) butter
- $^3/_4$ cup water
- 5 large eggs

Whipped Cream
- $3^1/_2$ cups heavy cream
- $^1/_2$ cup powdered sugar
- $^1/_4$ cup orange liqueur
- 3 tablespoons chocolate syrup

1. *For the cream puffs:* Arrange the oven racks to divide the oven into thirds. Preheat the oven to 450 degrees. You will need two large baking sheets lined with nonstick foil and a large star decorating tip.

2. Whisk the flour, baking powder, and salt in a small bowl. Bring the butter and water to a boil in a 3-quart saucepan over medium to high heat. Boil until the butter melts completely. Add the flour mixture all at once and stir until the mixture comes together. Stir constantly for 2 minutes.

3. Place the batter into the bowl of a mixer. With the mixer on medium speed, beat in the eggs one at a time until all of the eggs are incorporated. Place the batter into a pastry bag and pipe out 1-inch ball-shaped mounds onto the baking sheets. Bake for 10 minutes at 450 degrees, then reduce the oven to 350 degrees and continue baking for 10 more minutes.

4. *For the whipped cream:* In a bowl or mixer, place the cream, sugar, liqueur, and chocolate syrup. Mix on high until soft peaks form. To serve, cut each puff in half and place a dollop of cream inside each pastry.

Serves 6

Chocolate Cream Puffs

Fruit Tartlets

1²/₃ cups all-purpose flour
Large pinch of salt
¼ cup (½ stick) unsalted butter
⅓ cup sugar
1 egg

1–2 drops vanilla extract
3 fresh strawberries
3 fresh kiwis
1 whole pineapple, sliced
1 cup whipped cream

1. In a large bowl, sift together the flour and salt. Cut the butter into ½-inch cubes and add to the flour. Rub the butter into the flour using your fingertips until the mixture resembles bread crumbs.

2. Stir in the sugar and make a well in the center. Lightly beat the egg, combine it with the vanilla, and pour into the dry-ingredient well, slowly working everything together using a fork or flexible metal spatula. If the dough is too dry, sprinkle it with water until it just holds together.

3. Turn the dough out onto a lightly floured surface. Using the palm of your hand, smear the dough away from you repeatedly until it's smooth. Gather the dough into a ball and flatten it slightly. Wrap it in plastic wrap and chill in the refrigerator for 20 minutes before using.

Chef's Note: The quantity of pastry in this recipe is enough to line twelve 3-inch tart pans. If you're only making six tartlets, divide the pastry in half. Use one and seal the other in an airtight bag. Freeze for future use.

4. Preheat the oven to 375 degrees. Line six shallow 3-inch tart pans with pastry dough and bake for 15 minutes. Remove the shells from the oven and let them cool, then add the fruit and top with whipped cream. Serve cold.

Serves 6

Fruit Tartlets

9

Lisa Dahl, Andrea Di Luca, Dahl & Di Luca Ristorante Italiano and Cucina Rustica— Dahl & Di Luca

Lisa Dahl and Andrea Di Luca tell stories in unison, finish each other's sentences, and argue like sister and brother . . . or a married couple. The duo haven't been romantically involved since 2003, but they have been successful partners in the culinary world since opening their first restaurant, Dahl & Di Luca Ristorante Italiano, in 1995. Andrea fulfills the role of executive chef while Lisa is the executive sous chef, a relationship she calls a "marriage of sorts." Though their professional backgrounds are quite different, they both developed a love for cooking when they were teens.

Andrea was born in Rome. He began cooking at his uncle's restaurant when he was sixteen and admits he almost didn't stick with it after the first week, when he happened upon a cow leg hanging in the restaurant's refrigerator. He worked as an apprentice at Dietro la Cucina ("behind the stove," as Andrea translates it) in Rimini in northern Italy when he was nineteen; there he "learned from the old masters." In the 1970s he owned his own restaurant, Spaghetti Rocks, in Trastevere, Rome's hippest culinary neighborhood. "We had fifty or fifty-five seats and we'd have people, mothers with their children, waiting outside until midnight just to get in," says Andrea with a thick Italian accent. From there he worked in restaurants in Germany and Copenhagen before following his girlfriend to Providence, Rhode Island, in

1983. He spoke very little English and says he got his education "on the streets." He worked in restaurants in Rhode Island and Philadelphia before a fourteen-year stint as a sauté chef in San Francisco and Northern California; seven of those years were spent at Dalecio in Novato.

Lisa met Andrea at a party—he handed her his business card, and she told him she ate at Dalecio frequently. "I said to him, 'Maybe someday we'll have a restaurant together,'" Lisa remembers. This was in 1993 when she had a successful career selling high-end European footwear all over the West Coast. Born in Indianapolis, Lisa she says she started cooking when she was fifteen and remembers the great meals prepared by her mother, her grandmother, and especially her nanny, who liked to marry American classics with soul food. She spent time cooking in restaurants but, as a single mom, went into the fashion industry to raise her son, Justin—her keen fashion sense is still evident today. In 1994, when Justin was twenty-three, he was murdered in the Haight-Ashbury district in San Francisco. Lisa knew she had to leave the area, so she and Andrea relocated to Sedona, where Lisa had vacationed twice.

"I couldn't figure out why she wanted to take me to Arizona," says Andrea. "I thought it was all dusty and cactus. But when she brought me here I had goose bumps. Never in my life had I seen such beauty."

Lisa Dahl, executive sous chef, and Andrea Di Luca, executive chef, at Dahl & Di Luca Ristorante Italiano

Dahl & Di Luca Ristorante Italiano opened in a whirlwind fashion with very little time for training. "Andrea taught me the classic way and then I made each dish my own," says Lisa. The restaurant opened with a classic Italian menu featuring a northern flair but has since evolved into what Lisa calls "Italian classics with Lisa and Andrea's twists and respect to the old traditions." Andrea focuses on meat, seafood, and his handmade fresh pasta while Lisa's specialties are sauces (local favorites

The dining room at Dahl & Di Luca Ristorante Italiano

include her marinara, paradiso, and Bolognese sauces), soups, salads, and marinades. Lisa and Andrea call themselves "elegant peasant chefs" in style and say their philosophy is simple: "We cook what we like to eat—we put ourselves at the table."

Within one year of its opening, Dahl & Di Luca had been written up by one of Phoenix's top food critics; within two years *Bon Appétit* and *Gourmet* magazines were requesting recipes. The restaurant space is small with flaming torches on the outside, patio dining, and a large chandelier and linen-clad tables in the interior. In 2003 the duo opened their second restaurant, Cucina Rustica—Dahl & Di Luca, at Tequa Festival Marketplace in the Village of Oak Creek, in part because they wanted a bigger space for parties and groups. Andrea likes to say they opened the restaurant during a "momentary lapse of reason," while Lisa is more pragmatic. "I fell in love with the building and I wanted to branch out on cuisine," she says. "I wanted to cook more Mediterranean foods and touch on Southwest. What we have at Cucina is Mediterranean with a twist." (Think Portobello Ripieno stuffed with fresh spinach, chèvre, garlic, and herbs; or Penne Don Quixote, grilled chicken with sautéed mushrooms in a spicy chipotle cream sauce on penne pasta.)

Cucina Rustica has one of the loveliest interiors of any Sedona restaurant—it's divided into three distinct rooms, one with a large stone fireplace, another with a water fountain and stars on the ceiling, and a small back room with paintings of angels and saints on the walls. A note to anyone looking for romance: Cucina Rustica has a quiet corner booth in the water fountain room just perfect for celebrating anniversaries and Valentine's Day—ask for it when you make your reservation. Cucina also has an outdoor patio with two fireplaces, a trickling fountain, and red rock views—ideal for warm summer nights. Aside from the ambience, the house salad is one of the best you'll ever taste.

Both restaurants have a strong following with Sedona locals—Lisa says when Dahl & Di Luca first opened, they only served locals because tourists were unaccustomed to driving into West Sedona. Now they agree their clientele is fifty–fifty, and each restaurant stays incredibly busy, especially during high season. Don't even think about walking into Dahl & Di Luca on a Saturday in April—reservations are a must for this hot spot. It's nothing for Cucina to see 400 people per night while its smaller sibling serves up to 270. Both restaurants have unique wine lists with about a hundred bottles each. These aren't wines you will find in your local grocery store, but there is a wide variety of price ranges. Both locations have won *Wine Spectator* awards. In 2006 Lisa and Andrea opened Dahl & Di Luca A'Roma, a gourmet food, wine, and gift shop next door to Cucina Rustica, to "make the home cook look like a pro," says Lisa. A'Roma also sells sandwiches, salads, desserts, and platters.

So what keeps Lisa and Andrea, both of whom spend time in the kitchen five to six days a week, ticking? Lisa says they have been blessed from above, referring to her son and Andrea's parents, who passed away while he was still a child. "We were really visionary in Sedona, we took chances and we got the support we needed," Lisa says. "We started with no money but we had a blessed mission. Our loved ones are guiding our path."

Chef Dahl's Tricks of the Trade

"When you are entertaining at home, you can do it without a lot of fuss—you can throw parties that look like you've been cooking for days when you've only been in the kitchen for an hour, especially if you stick with Mediterranean cuisine. Keep your colors vivid and platter everything separately so people know what they are eating. Use marinades and keep everything looking like it just came off the vine—less is more."

Chef Di Luca's Tricks of the Trade

"Make sure you are in the mood for the food you are cooking. Buy and cook the right ingredients and enjoy your time in the kitchen. Everyone is in such a rush—slow down when you are in the kitchen. Don't drown your food in sauce, and make sure your pasta is al dente."

At Home

Chef Dahl says she likes to cook at home, but she considers each restaurant her home kitchen and prefers cooking for her staff—she's also a big fan of eating out on her days off. "I really only cook at home when I'm throwing a party—for my last birthday I cooked for three days. But we are only closed two days a year so I eat in our restaurants the nights I work. I also like to try out new recipes on our staff. I've been eating in our two restaurants for twelve years, and I can honestly say I'm never bored with the cuisine. This is my dining room."

Chef Di Luca says that when he's alone on his days off, he'll eat fast food and junk food, but when his wife is around it's another story. "If my wife wants a friend to come over for dinner, the first thing I do is make a mess all over the kitchen [laughs]. I do like to visit other restaurants to keep up on trends, and at home I cook a lot of seafood."

Dahl & Di Luca Ristorante Italiano
2321 West Highway 89A, West Sedona
928-282-5219
www.dahlanddiluca.com

Cucina Rustica—Dahl & Di Luca
7000 Highway 179, Oak Creek
928-284-3010
www.cucinarustica.com

One of the dining rooms at Cucina Rustica

Lisa's Grilled Portobello Mushroom Ripieno Stuffed with Spinach and Chèvre

Recipes

Lisa's Grilled Portobello Mushroom Ripieno Stuffed with Spinach and Chèvre

Marinade

- 2 cups olive oil
- 1 cup balsamic vinegar
- 1 cup low-sodium soy sauce
- 1/2 cup Marsala wine (optional)
- 3–5 cloves fresh garlic
- 8–10 sprigs fresh thyme
- 1/2 teaspoon kosher salt
- 1/2 teaspoon coarse-ground black pepper

Stuffing

- 6 large portobello mushrooms
- 1 10-ounce package frozen chopped spinach
- 1 pound button mushrooms
- 1/2 large sweet yellow onion
- 3 cloves garlic
- 1/3–1/2 cup olive oil
- 1/2 teaspoon kosher salt (to taste)
- 1/2 teaspoon black pepper
- 6 ounces crumbled chèvre
- 1/3 cup unseasoned bread crumbs
- 1/4 cup high-quality Parmesan cheese

1. *For the marinade:* Combine all of the marinade ingredients.

2. *For the stuffing:* Carefully de-stem the portobellos and set aside the stems for stuffing. Cover the mushrooms with marinade and set aside at room temperature for 4 hours, turning over after 2 hours.

3. Cook the frozen spinach as directed on the package. Drain, cool, and set aside.

4. Clean the button mushrooms. Coarsely chop all of the button mushrooms and reserved Portobello stems in a food processor, then set aside. Finely chop the onion in the food processor and set aside. Chop the garlic finely and set aside.

5. Heat 1/3 cup olive oil, add the onion, chopped button mushrooms, and chopped Portobello stems. Cook over a high flame until lightly caramelized (2 to 3 minutes) to draw out the moisture. When the mixture becomes golden brown, sprinkle with salt and pepper to taste. Lower the flame, add the chopped garlic, and sauté until

fully cooked but not burned. Remove the mixture from the heat and cool in a bowl at room temperature. Add the drained spinach, crumble on the goat cheese (chèvre), and toss lightly. Add in the bread crumbs followed by the Parmesan. Toss lightly. Set aside.

6. Drain the portobello mushrooms, making sure all of the oil is removed. Preheat a gas grill to a medium flame—any higher will char the mushrooms. Grill the portobellos center-side down for 2 to 3 minutes then turn them over, continuing to score both sides evenly like a steak until the water has drawn out and each mushroom is nicely seared. Remove the mushrooms from the grill into a casserole or sheet pan center-side up.

7. Lightly stuff each mushroom with the spinach–chèvre mixture without packing too tightly.

8. Preheat the oven to 350 degrees. Bake the stuffed mushrooms for 15 minutes or until browned on top. You can always broil for a moment or two if additional browning is desired. Serve as an entree or slightly cool and cut into quarters for appetizers.

Serves 6 as main course or up to 24 as appetizer

Spaghetti alla Carbonara

Spaghetti alla Carbonara

5 ounces pancetta, diced
2 medium yellow onions, diced
3 tablespoons olive oil
Salt and ground black pepper to taste

¼ cup whipping cream
1½–2 pounds cooked spaghetti
4 organic egg yolks, whipped
1 cup fresh-grated Parmesan cheese

In a large frying pan over medium heat, sauté the diced pancetta and onions with the olive oil and a dash of salt until golden brown. Add the cream. In a mixing bowl toss the spaghetti with whipped yolks and Parmesan. Add to fry pan mixture. Sprinkle with fresh-ground black pepper.

Serves 6–8

Vitella alla Romana

2 pounds veal (scaloppine *or* medallions)

2 tablespoons olive oil

5 cloves garlic, chopped

½ cup chopped parsley

6 leaves basil

2 tablespoons (¼ stick) butter

1 pound sliced shiitake mushrooms

2 cups Marsala wine

Salt and pepper to taste

Sauté the veal with the olive oil over high heat; turn it over, add the garlic, and continue cooking until it's a golden brown. Add the parsley, basil, butter, mushrooms, and Marsala wine and reduce heat to a simmer. Allow to thicken until the sauce is silky and transparent. Salt and pepper to taste.

Serves 6–8

Vitella alla Romana

Petto di Pollo Piccata

Petto di Pollo Piccata

3 tablespoons olive oil

6–8 8-ounce chicken breasts

½ cup capers

2 tablespoons (¼ stick) butter

Salt and pepper to taste

2 tablespoons lemon juice

2 cups Chardonnay or Pinot Grigio
  wine

½ cup chopped fresh Italian parsley

Heat the oil in a large skillet over high heat. Sauté the chicken with the capers, butter, salt, pepper, lemon juice, and wine until it's golden and crispy. Garnish with the parsley.

Serves 6–8

Italian Cream Cake

½ cup (1 stick) unsalted butter,
  softened
2 cups sugar
½ cup canola oil
5 egg yolks
½ teaspoon vanilla extract
1 cup sifted cake flour

1 cup sifted all-purpose flour
1¼ teaspoons baking powder
1 cup buttermilk
½ cup shredded coconut
¾ cup chopped pecans
5 egg whites

1. Preheat a conventional oven to 350 degrees; if you're using a convection oven, preheat it to 325 degrees. Grease and flour three 8-inch metal cake pans.

2. Cream together the softened butter and sugar, add the canola oil, and blend until creamy. Scrape down the bowl. Add the egg yolks one at a time, beating after each addition. Add the vanilla and beat until creamy.

3. Combine the flours and baking powder and add to the yolk mixture. Add the buttermilk. Once this is blended, add the coconut and pecans and beat on medium high for 2 minutes.

4. Whip the egg whites until soft peaks form. Fold the whites into the yolk mixture.

5. Pour the batter into the prepared pans and bake for 50 minutes or until an inserted knife comes out clean. Cool the cakes slightly, then remove them from the pans and let them cool thoroughly before icing.

Cream Cheese Icing

1 pound cream cheese, softened
½ cup (1 stick) butter, softened

3 cups sifted powdered sugar
Dash of lemon juice

Beat the cream cheese until soft and fluffy. Add the softened butter and beat until well blended. On low, add the sifted sugar to your desired sweetness. Add a dash of lemon juice if desired. Beat the icing on low-medium speed until smooth and fluffy.

Use this icing to frost all three layers of cake. Stack the layers one atop the other. Garnish the sides of the cake with additional toasted coconut and pecans.

Serves 6–8

Italian Cream Cake

10

Steven Bernstein and Yavapai Restaurant

As you sit in front of the floor-to-ceiling windows at Yavapai Restaurant, so close to the sheer red rock cliffs and spires of Boynton Canyon you feel like you could touch them, it occurs to you that there are few restaurants on earth with a view that can bring a hushed reverence to your table. This writer has only experienced the feeling on one other occasion, at Château Eza, 1,500 feet above the Mediterranean on the border of France and Monaco. Dining at Yavapai, located at Enchantment Resort, is a sensory experience, from the view to the sound of classical music softly playing in the background to the feel of the leather-covered menus to the taste of the southwestern-influenced Continental cuisine. It's no wonder executive chef Steven Bernstein has called the Four Diamond Yavapai—named after a local Native American tribe—his second home since 2001.

Steven, the youngest of four, grew up in New Orleans, where his dad worked as an architect. His parents often took him out to dinner with them—he says he remembers brunch at upscale hotels at an early age. He started cooking as a teenager. When he turned twenty he moved to Phoenix and worked at some of the area's premier resorts before deciding to attend the Culinary Institute of America in New York. He graduated with honors in 1992 and took positions in New Orleans, Phoenix, and even aboard the *Mississippi Queen* steamboat before settling at Miraval resort in Tucson in 1997. There he learned the art of spa cuisine, a skill that helped him land the job at Enchantment. The resort's destination spa, Mii amo, consistently ranks as one of the best spas in the world in publications such as *Travel + Leisure* (world's best spa in 2007), *Condé Nast Traveler* (whose readers named Enchantment one of the world's 721 best places to stay in 2008), and Zagat guides.

"I spent a lot of time at Mii amo during my first four years here," says Steven, who bears a slight resemblance in face and cadence to Bruce Willis. "We went from doing 30 covers a day to 200. We provide everyone at Mii amo with calorie charts, and the guests are always surprised to see how healthy the meals are and how good everything tastes. It's very simple and satisfying—smaller portions but with the most flavor."

Steven oversees the resort's three restaurants: Mii amo Café (breakfast, lunch, and dinner), Yavapai (breakfast, lunch, and dinner), and Ti Gavo (pronounced *de gahvo*—lunch and dinner), a more casual lounge that still comes with Yavapai's stunning views. Mii amo Café offers weekly cooking classes and tea demonstrations. The restaurants serve only all-natural meats, fish flown in from Hawaii five times a week, and a variety of fresh produce, including mushrooms from Oregon and tomatoes and greens from Arizona. Steven's food philosophy is simple: Quality is number one.

"I have no boundaries here—I buy the food from where I want at the level of quality I want. I know where everything comes from," he says. "At Enchantment quality means more than saving a dime—we are a destination with travelers coming from all over the world to stay with us and dine with us. They are well traveled and they know their food—anything but the best isn't acceptable."

Steven Bernstein, executive chef at Yavapai Restaurant

Favorite menu items at Yavapai include the rack of Colorado lamb, buffalo tenderloin, and Pasole Soup. Adventurous eaters enjoy red abalone and wild game such as venison and antelope. Steven's team of more than fifty goes through four cases of avocados every day to make fresh guacamole—everything, from the salsa to the ice cream and desserts, is made from scratch. Locals and travelers alike rave about Yavapai's Sunday brunch with live jazz, which includes a seafood station, lamb, and caviar. Yavapai's wine list includes 900 bottles with an inventory of 12,000, earning the restaurant numerous awards from *Wine Spectator*. During the warmer months you can dine on Yavapai's terrace with the resort's immaculately manicured lawns, discreet, one-story adobe casitas, and blue swimming pools spread out below.

Enchantment opened in 1987 on seventy acres of a private homestead in Boynton Canyon just southwest of Sedona. Its focus was on tennis, and the resort still boasts seven courts. Local Apache believe First Woman, the founder of their tribe, was born in the canyon. Several times each year the Yavapai-Apache return to the canyon at sunrise to hold sacred ceremonies, including one honoring First Woman. The 220-room resort embraces its unique location, according to Annika Jackson, vice president and managing director.

"The Native American culture has a big influence on Enchantment," she says. "We are proud of our heritage, and our guests are interested in it. We have a Native American program director on staff, and we host lectures, Hopi dancers, Navajo flute music, storytelling, and medicine walks. Over 50 percent of our guests are repeat visitors, and while they certainly come for the food, the spa, and the canyon, they also come for the cultural experience."

The 24,000-square-foot Mii amo, a Native American term meaning "journey" or "passage," plays a major role at Enchantment—the spa is only open to Enchantment guests or those who choose to stay at one of Mii amo's sixteen rooms and suites for three-, four-, and seven-day inclusive programs. Enchantment also offers a kids' program, a 12,000-square-foot meeting village, a par-three golf course and putting green, and mountain bike rentals.

Yavapai Restaurant at Enchantment Resort

The dining room at Yavapai Restaurant at Enchantment Resort

Chef Bernstein's Tricks of the Trade

"A good set of knives and All-Clad pots will cost you some money, but they will last. Be creative when it comes to meals, look to see what's out there. Try exploring with grains rather than meat—bulk grains are fun to cook with, and they all cook differently. I love risotto, couscous, and bulgur wheat. You might mess up a few times, but that's how you'll learn. Some of the best dishes come from accidents."

At Home

Chef Bernstein says he'd rather cook at home than eat out, which is probably why his twelve-year-old has developed a taste for rack of lamb. "My partner is a great cook—she learned it from me, but sometimes she's better than me [laughs]. I like to grill—I have two grills in the yard—and I like to create from what I have in the refrigerator. Sometimes it's a crazy meal but it turns out to be the best thing. I don't like to be rushed. It takes me a couple of hours to make anything."

Yavapai Restaurant at Enchantment Resort
525 Boynton Canyon Road, Sedona
928-282-2900
www.enchantmentresort.com

Recipes

Banana-Stuffed French Toast

Toast
2 cups cream cheese, softened
6 bananas, peeled and sliced
2 teaspoons brown sugar
1 teaspoon banana extract or flavoring
1 teaspoon vanilla extract
16 pieces Texas toast
Butter or oil, for cooking

Batter
10 eggs
1 quart milk
$\frac{1}{4}$ cup ground cinnamon
1 cup sugar
1 teaspoon ground nutmeg

Crust
6 cups pecans
6 cups cornflake crumbs

1. *For the toast:* Place the cream cheese in a bowl; add the bananas, brown sugar, banana extract, and vanilla. Fold gently until mixed well. Spread approximately ½ cup of filling on a piece of Texas toast and top with another piece of toast. Repeat this with the remaining pieces of bread until the filling is gone. When you're finished, place the toast in the refrigerator for approximately 15 minutes.

2. *For the batter:* Place the eggs in a bowl and whisk until incorporated. Add the milk, cinnamon, sugar, and nutmeg. Mix well and refrigerate.

3. *For the crust:* Place the pecans in a food processor and pulse until coarsely ground. Add to the cornflake crumbs in a medium bowl and mix well.

4. *Assembly:* Dip each sandwich into the batter and dredge in the crust mixture. Add butter or oil to a heated griddle or sauté pan. Brown the pieces on each side for approximately 3 to 4 minutes or until they're warm in the center. Cut them in half and serve with butter, powdered sugar, and your favorite syrup.

Serves 8

Banana-Stuffed French Toast

Chipotle-Dusted Sea Scallops with Bulgur Corn Pilaf and Warm Tomatillo Salsa

Tomatillo Salsa (makes 3 cups)
- 1 pound tomatillos, husks removed
- 1 jalapeño, stem removed
- 1 tablespoon plus 1 teaspoon olive oil, divided
- 1 cup diced red onion
- 1 cup diced poblano chile
- 1/2 cup diced red pepper
- 1/4 cup chopped green onions
- 1 tablespoon minced garlic
- 1/2 bunch cilantro
- 2 tablespoons lime juice
- Salt and pepper to taste
- 1 teaspoon honey (optional)

Bulgur Wheat Corn Pilaf
- 2 cups bulgur wheat
- 2 cups boiling water or vegetable stock
- 2 cups fresh corn kernels
- 1 tablespoon olive oil
- 1/4 cup diced red onion
- 1/4 cup diced celery
- 1/4 cup diced carrot
- Salt and pepper to taste

Chipotle-Dusted Sea Scallops
- 32 U-10 dry scallops
- Chipotle powder, for dusting (available in gourmet food markets)
- Salt and pepper to taste
- Olive oil, for cooking

Chipotle-Dusted Sea Scallops with Bulgur Corn Pilaf and Warm Tomatillo Salsa

1. *For the salsa:* Preheat the oven to 400 degrees. Toss the tomatillos with the jalapeño in 1 teaspoon of the olive oil. Place on a baking sheet and roast in the oven for 10 to 12 minutes until browned and soft. Remove from the oven, but maintain the oven temperature.

2. Heat the remaining tablespoon of olive oil in a large frying pan. Add the onion, poblanos, red pepper, green onions, and garlic. Sweat until the vegetables are translucent. Add the roasted tomatillos and jalapeño and continue cooking for 3 to 5 minutes. Place all of the ingredients in a blender with the cilantro and lime and blend until semi-smooth. Season with salt and pepper. If a sweeter balance is desired, then add honey. This will balance the tartness of the salsa. Set aside.

3. *For the bulgur pilaf:* Place the bulgur wheat in a bowl and pour in the boiling water or vegetable stock. Cover with plastic wrap and let sit for 20 minutes or until all of the water is absorbed. Fluff with a fork and set aside.

4. Place the corn kernels on a baking sheet and place in the 400-degree oven for 5 to 8 minutes or until they're golden brown and soft. Remove and set aside. Maintain the oven temperature.

5. Heat the olive oil in a large saucepan. Add the onion, celery, and carrot. Sweat for 3 to 5 minutes until the vegetables are soft. Add the corn and bulgur wheat, stirring until incorporated. Keep warm.

6. *For the sea scallops:* Season the scallops with the chipotle powder, salt, and pepper. (If powder is not available, use dried chipotles, grinding them in a spice grinder until they become a powder.)

7. Heat olive oil in a large sauté pan. When it's hot, add the scallops and sear on both sides for 1 to 2 minutes. To achieve medium doneness, place in the 400-degree oven for 2 to 4 minutes.

Chef's Note: Using a nonstick pan to sear the scallops will prevent them from sticking. In this case, you can use less oil—reducing calories. This is known as dry sauté.

8. *Assembly:* Place ½ cup of the pilaf in the center of each plate or large bowl. Ladle ¼ cup of the salsa around the perimeter. Place four scallops on top of the salsa, spreading them around the pilaf.

Serves 8

Coq au Vin, Cipollinis, Mushrooms, and Turkey Bacon with Brown Rice and Cabernet Jus

Cabernet Jus (makes 2 cups)
- 1 tablespoon olive oil
- 1 cup sliced shallots
- 1 cup sliced button mushrooms
- 1 teaspoon minced garlic
- 10 cracked black peppercorns
- 1 bay leaf
- 2 sprigs fresh thyme
- 2 cups Cabernet Sauvignon
- 3 cups veal stock (or substitute beef broth or a purchased stock)
- Salt and pepper to taste

Coq au Vin
- 8 ounces turkey bacon, for garnish
- 24 cipollini onions, peeled
- 4 tablespoons olive oil
- Salt and pepper to taste
- 32 whole cremini mushrooms, stems removed
- 2 tablespoons chopped parsley
- 8 4-ounce boneless and skinless chicken breasts
- 4 cups cooked brown rice

1. Preheat the oven to 400 degrees.

2. *For the Cabernet Jus:* Heat the olive oil in a saucepan. Add the shallots, mushrooms, garlic, peppercorns, bay leaf, and thyme. Sweat slowly until the vegetables are soft. Add the wine and simmer until reduced by half. Add the stock and continue simmering until the stock is reduced by half. Strain the sauce and season with salt and pepper to taste. Keep warm.

3. *For the Coq au Vin:* Begin by making the turkey bacon garnish. Slice the bacon lengthwise very thinly. Place on a baking sheet and bake until it's crispy, about 7 to 10 minutes. Remove from the oven, but maintain the oven temperature.

4. Toss the cipollini onions with 2 tablespoons of olive oil, salt, and pepper. Roast on a baking tray in the 400-degree oven for 8 to 10 minutes or until they're golden brown and soft. Remove from the oven, but maintain the oven temperature.

5. Heat 2 more tablespoons of olive oil in a large sauté pan. Add the cremini mushrooms. Sauté until the mushrooms begin to soften. Add the cipollinis and Cabernet Jus. Cook until the sauce reaches a simmer. Finish with parsley, salt, and pepper. Set aside.

Coq au Vin, Cipollinis, Mushrooms, and Turkey Bacon with Brown Rice and Cabernet Jus

6. *For the chicken:* Season the breasts with salt and pepper. Heat olive oil in a pan and brown them on both sides. Place the chicken in the 400-degree oven for 5 to 7 minutes or until cooked. Let the breasts rest for 3 to 5 minutes.

7. *Assembly:* Place ½ cup of cooked brown rice in center of each plate. Place a chicken breast on top of the rice. Spoon three cipollinis and four mushrooms around the chicken. Spoon about 3 tablespoons of Cabernet Jus over the chicken and garnish with crispy turkey bacon.

Serves 8

Olive-Crusted Rack of Colorado Lamb and Potato Tart with Rosemary Jus

Grilled Vegetable and Potato Tart

1 eggplant, peeled

1 zucchini

1 yellow squash

4 portobello mushrooms

Olive oil, for seasoning

Salt and pepper to taste

2 whole eggs

1 cup heavy cream

4 pounds large Yukon Gold
   potatoes, peeled

Vegetable spray

4 cups shredded Manchego cheese

1 cup chopped roasted tomatoes
   (available in most markets, usually
   in a jar with oil)

Olive Crust

4 cups sliced olives

2 cups bread crumbs

Rosemary Jus

1 tablespoon olive oil

1 cup sliced shallots

1 cup sliced mushrooms

1 teaspoon minced garlic

$1/2$ cup chopped tomatoes

2 sprigs fresh thyme

2 tablespoons chopped fresh
   rosemary

10 cracked peppercorns

1 bay leaf

$1\frac{1}{2}$ cups white wine

3 cups veal stock

1 tablespoon butter

Lamb

8 lamb racks (approximately 12
   ounces each, 4 bones)

$1/2$ cup Dijon mustard

Olive oil, for cooking

1. *For the tart:* Preheat the oven to 325 degrees. Slice the eggplant, zucchini, and yellow squash about ⅛ inch thick. Season the vegetable slices and portobellos with oil, salt, and pepper. Cook the slices on the grill for 1 to 2 minutes on each side, until slightly cooked. Grill the mushrooms for 3 minutes on each side, constantly turning, until soft. Cool down immediately.

2. Make a custard using the eggs, cream, salt, and pepper.

3. Peel the potatoes and place them in cold water to prevent oxidation. Coat a 12x18-inch sheet pan with vegetable spray and line with parchment paper. Slice potatoes on a slicer or mandoline to approximately ⅛ inch thick. Layer the pan with potato slices, slightly overlapping. Season with salt and pepper. Repeat this process to create a second layer of potatoes. Slice the mushrooms into three pieces each

Olive-Crusted Rack of Colorado Lamb and Potato Tart with Rosemary Jus

(twelve pieces total). Layer the grilled vegetable slices, alternating each kind, to cover the pan. Be sure to only use six portobello slices per layer. Sprinkle 2 cups of the cheese and ½ cup of the tomatoes over the vegetable layer. Spoon 3 to 4 tablespoons of custard over the layer. This will help the tart to bind during the baking process. Repeat the process with another layer of potatoes. Then repeat the process with the vegetables, remaining cheese, and remaining tomatoes. Finally, finish with two more layers of potatoes. Be sure to season each layer with salt and pepper and drizzle some custard between the layers. Coat the top layer with vegetable spray and cover with parchment paper.

4. Place another pan (of the same size) over the top of the tart. Weigh it down with a brick wrapped in aluminum foil. Bake at 325 degrees for about 1 hour and 10 minutes or until the potatoes are tender. When the tart is done, carefully remove the brick, top pan, and paper. Let it cool; it's best to chill it down overnight. This tart will keep for up to 4 days in the refrigerator.

Chef's Note: The custard will not be visible—it's just lightly drizzled between layers to keep them together. To cut the tart when it's cold, flip the pan upside down on a cutting board and remove the bottom sheet of parchment paper. Cut to your preferred size.

5. *For the olive crust:* Preheat the oven to 250 degrees. Place the olives on a baking pan and bake for about 1½ to 2 hours or until they're dried out and crispy. Place the olives and bread crumbs in a food processor. Blend until the mixture is a medium texture—not too coarse, but not too smooth. Set aside. This crust mixture will keep for up to 2 weeks in the refrigerator.

6. *For the rosemary jus:* Heat a small saucepan over a medium-high flame. Add the oil, shallots, mushrooms, garlic, and tomatoes. Sweat the vegetables for 3 to 5 minutes until soft. Add the herbs, peppercorns, and bay leaf. Add the wine and simmer until the pan is almost dry, 20 to 25 minutes. Add the veal stock and reduce by half, to about 2 cups. Strain and season with salt and pepper. Finish with the butter.

7. *For the lamb:* Preheat the oven to 375 degrees. Season the racks with salt and pepper. In a medium-hot sauté pan, add the oil and sear the lamb racks on all sides until they're brown. Place in the oven for 12 to 15 minutes until medium rare. Let the meat rest for 5 minutes; reduce the oven temperature to 350 degrees. Brush each rack with 1 tablespoon of Dijon mustard, and crust with the olive mixture. Place in the oven for 2 to 3 minutes until the crust is browned.

8. *Assembly:* Cut each piece of warm tart in half, placing one piece on top of the other in the center of a plate. Cut each lamb rack into two pieces; interlock the bones to make the rack stand up against the tart. Finish with 3 to 4 tablespoons of rosemary jus. Garnish with your favorite baby vegetable and serve.

Serves 8

Pan-Seared Sea Bass with White Bean Puree, Five-Onion Ragout, Parsley Cream, and Veal Jus

White Bean Puree (makes about
    4 cups)
    4 cups cooked white beans (canned
        beans can be substituted)
    ½ cup mascarpone cheese
    ¼ cup heavy cream
    1 teaspoon salt
    ½ teaspoon pepper

Five-Onion Ragout
    2 tablespoons olive oil
    1 cup julienned red onion
    1 cup julienned sweet yellow onion
        (Vidalia or Maui onions can be
        substituted)
    1 cup sliced green onions (slice on
        bias)
    1 cup julienned leeks, white parts
        only

1 cup sliced shallots
1 tablespoon minced garlic
2 teaspoons fresh thyme
½ cup red wine
1 cup veal stock or purchased beef
    broth

Parsley Cream (makes 2 cups)
    2 cups heavy cream
    2 cups finely chopped Italian parsley
    Salt and pepper to taste

Sea Bass
    8 4-ounce sea bass fillets
    Salt and pepper to taste
    Flour, for dredging
    Olive oil, for cooking

1. *For the puree:* Place the cooked white beans in a food processor with the mascarpone and cream. Puree until smooth. Season with salt and pepper.

2. *For the ragout:* Heat a medium sauté pan. Add the olive oil, onions, and garlic. Cook the onions slowly, for 10 to 15 minutes, until they're translucent and caramelized. Add the fresh thyme and red wine. Cook for 2 minutes and add the veal stock (or beef broth). Cook down for another 3 to 4 minutes and season with salt and pepper. Set aside.

3. *For the parsley cream:* Place the cream and parsley in a small sauce pot and cook until the mixture thickens, about 5 to 7 minutes. The consistency should coat the back of a spoon. Season with salt and pepper.

Pan-Seared Sea Bass with White Bean Puree, Five-Onion Ragout, Parsley Cream, and Veal Jus

4. *For the sea bass:* Preheat the oven to 375 dgrees. Season the fish with salt and pepper. Dredge in flour and place in a medium to hot sauté pan with olive oil. Brown the fish for about 2 minutes on each side. Place in the oven for about 4 to 6 minutes until cooked to a medium temperature. The fish should be cooked, but the center should be slightly translucent. Keep warm.

5. *Assembly:* Place ½ cup of bean puree in the center of each plate. Add ¼ cup of onion ragout on top of the puree. Place a sea bass fillet over the ragout, then drizzle about 2 tablespoons of parsley cream on top of the fish and around the plate.

Serves 8

11

Michael Merilli
and Adobe Grand Villas

Michael Merilli, executive chef and general manager of Adobe Grand Villas, will be the first to admit that chefs don't always have the best eating habits . . . particularly not those chefs hailing from New Orleans. Michael spent sixteen years cooking in the Big Easy and owned two restaurants, Gauthier Market Cafe and the Abita Quail Farm, before coming to Sedona in 2002 to help open Adobe Grand. He recalls working with well-known chefs including Gerard Maras, Susan Spicer, John Neal, and Emeril Lagasse. "After we'd do a wedding, Emeril and I would head to Burger King," he says with a laugh.

Michael misses New Orleans, but he's continuing a love affair with Sedona that began when he spent a month hiking in Red Rock Country on vacation. Three months later he sold his restaurant in New Orleans and migrated west. Now he works six days a week, sometimes sixteen hours a day, at the luxurious Four Diamond Adobe Grand Villas—a B&B, inn, and resort owned by Stuart and Ilene Berman (the couple celebrated their fortieth anniversary at about the same time Adobe Grand opened to its first guests in June 2004). The property boasts fifteen themed rooms, each ranging in size from 850 to 2,000 square feet, the largest rooms in Sedona. A stay at Adobe is unlike most B&Bs—take it from someone who knows. The oversize king beds are triple-sheeted and require a stepstool to get into; the enormous bathrooms have double sinks, a whirlpool tub for two, a fireplace, and walk-in waterfall showers with artisan showerheads. Stuart and Ilene's son, Steven, designed each room and hand-carved every last bed and huge door, including the covered-wagon bed and a door with a built-in waterwheel in the Wagon Wheel room. Each afternoon the innkeepers come into the rooms to turn on music and begin baking fresh bread in

Michael Merilli, executive chef and general manager at Adobe Grand Villas

the kitchenette—when guests return from a day of hiking or gallery-hopping, they are greeted with the smell of warm bread and the sounds of Andrea Bocelli. Beds are turned down each evening with a piece of chocolate, and all in-room snacks and refreshments are complimentary. Adobe Grand also has a couples spa with a steam room on-site. It's no wonder guests don't show up for breakfast until late morning.

"We owned another inn in Sedona when we first moved here and, when the chef would arrive at 7:00 a.m., there would be a line of people waiting for breakfast and eager to begin their day," recalls Stuart. "When we opened Adobe we started breakfast at 7:00 a.m., but no one arrived. They didn't show up at 8:00 a.m., either. We finally changed our breakfast hours to 8:30 to 10:00 a.m. because people just weren't leaving their rooms. The room is part of the Sedona experience as opposed to being just a room."

And for those who simply can't bring themselves to leave the red rock views from their balconies or private gardens, or the views of the fireplace from their sumptuous beds (each room has two fireplaces—one near the foot of the bed and one in the bathroom), Michael will serve his four-course breakfast in guest rooms. Breakfast is also served in the B&B's great room, complete with bronze sculptures of cowboys and Indians, iron chandeliers, wood-beamed ceilings, and fresh flowers, or they can dine alfresco near Adobe's flower gardens and swimming pool. Guest favorites include the Bread Pudding French Toast with Caramelized Banana Syrup, Louisiana Crab Cakes with Poached Eggs and Chipotle Hollandaise, and Grillades and Grits—Michael's marriage of the Southwest

Entrance to the Adobe Grand Villas courtyard

Fireplace in the gathering room at the Adobe Grand Villas

and New Orleans, which includes slow-roasted beef in a Creole sauce served over grits with a poached egg.

"I think comfort food is always the best," says Michael, a bear of a man with curly dark hair. "It can fulfill any situation. Here at Adobe Grand we try to make guests happy—we'll get them anything they want. I'd have to say my strangest request was for eight crème brûlées and candles for a couple staying in our White Dove room."

Presentation is important at the Adobe Grand—Michael likes to garnish plates with rose petals or organic flowers grown on-site as well as cocoa powder and powdered sugar on sweet dishes, or chili powder on savory plates. While guests have been known to stay at Adobe for up to fifteen days, Michael takes pride in ensuring that they do not receive the same breakfast twice during their stay. He admits he doesn't know what he's going to make until he wakes up that morning. He doesn't follow recipes very often, either, though he collects cookbooks because it's "fun to see what other people do." He likes to try out new flavors and new menu items on guests during the evening hors d'oeuvres hour.

Michael also serves private dinners in the evening by reservation only and with at least six hours' notice. The dinner menu changes seasonally and could include Pretzel-Crusted Salmon with Creole Mustard Beurre Blanc or Cheese-Stuffed Filet Mignon with Bordelaise Sauce. The dinner menu generally includes three appetizers, two salads, five to six entrees, and two to three desserts. On Valentine's Day, Michael has been known to serve a five-course dinner, with each course incorporating chocolate. Both breakfast and dinner are open to nonguests during the slower months and by reservation. During the dinner hour Michael acts as chef, server, and dishwasher, something he absolutely loves. "The joy is the immediate gratification that comes with knowing guests are enjoying their meals," he says. "I originally went to school to be an elementary school teacher, but eighteen years is too long to wait to see how your students turn out."

Chef Merilli's Tricks of the Trade

"Parchment paper can be a lifesaver—use it on top of cookie sheets to save scrubbing. Never underestimate quality ingredients, and be careful where you shop. If you are working with quality food, it doesn't need to be covered by heavy sauces—it will stand on its own. Buy from reputable markets and look for organics. When buying fish, the eyes should be clear, the flesh should be firm, and it shouldn't smell like fish. Meat should be red and marbled with fat. Smell and feel your produce—it shouldn't feel waxy."

At Home

Chef Merilli is a follower of the slow-food movement, and it shows in the food he prepares at home. "I stick to comfort foods. I like to throw something together before I go to work and let it simmer all day. Monday is red beans and rice day. In New Orleans the Creole women would do laundry on Mondays, so there was no time to be in the kitchen. They would let the red beans and rice cook all day."

Adobe Grand Villas
35 Hozoni, Sedona
928-203-7616
www.adobegrandvillas.com

Recipes

Louisiana Crab Cakes with Poached Eggs and Chipotle Hollandaise

Crab Cakes

- 1 pound jumbo lump or lump crab-meat (Louisiana preferred)
- 1/2 cup finely diced red onion
- 1/4 cup small-diced red pepper
- 1/4 cup small-diced green pepper
- 1/2 cup diced celery
- 1 tablespoon chopped fresh garlic
- 1/4 cup sliced green onions
- 1 small pear, diced
- 2 tablespoons chopped fresh parsley or cilantro
- 2 tablespoons honey
- 2 tablespoons Dijon mustard
- 2 tablespoons fresh lemon juice
- 2 large eggs
- 1 teaspoon hot sauce or chili paste (optional)
- 1/4 cup mayonnaise
- 3/4 cup bread crumbs
- 1 tablespoon Creole seasoning
- Salt and pepper to taste

Chipotle Hollandaise

- 3 egg yolks at room temperature
- 2 tablespoons lemon juice
- 1/4 teaspoon salt
- Dash of cayenne pepper
- 3/4 cup (1 1/2 sticks) butter
- 1/2 chipotle pepper, diced
- 1 tablespoon chipotle adobo sauce

Egg Wash

- 3 eggs
- 1/2 cup milk

Breading

- 1 1/2 cups bread crumbs
- 1 tablespoon Creole seasoning

Assembly

- 1 cup flour
- 1 cup peanut or canola oil
- 6–8 eggs

1. *For the crab cakes:* Choose a high-quality crabmeat; jumbo or lump work best. Pick through the meat to ensure that no shells exist. Place the crabmeat and remaining ingredients into a bowl. Gently mix so that everything's incorporated, without breaking the crab up too much. Form into 1/3- to 1/2-cup balls and refrigerate for an hour.

2. *For the hollandaise:* Put the egg yolks, lemon juice, salt, and cayenne into the jar of a blender. Heat the butter in small pan or microwave. Skim off the white whey that forms on top of the butter and discard. Cover the blender and whirl at high speed for 2 or 3 seconds. Remove the blender cover and at high speed pour in the

Louisiana Crab Cakes with Poached Eggs and Chipotle Hollandaise

hot butter in a thin, steady stream. It will take about 30 seconds. Gently stir in the chipotle and adobo sauce and keep the mixture in a double boiler until you're ready to use it.

3. *For the egg wash:* Whisk together the eggs and milk.

4. *For the breading:* Mix together the bread crumbs and Creole seasoning.

5. *Assembly:* Remove the crab cakes from the refrigerator and gently flatten them into patties. Dip each into plain flour, then into the egg wash, and finish by patting them in the bread crumb mix. Heat 1 cup of quality oil such as peanut or canola in a large, deep skillet, preferably cast-iron. Sauté the crab cakes until they're golden brown on both sides. Top each crab cake with a poached egg and dollop with hollandaise.

Serves 4–6

Sedona Sunrise: Fried Eggs Over Seared Polenta with Wild Mushroom Ragout

Polenta
  2 cups milk or half-and-half
  2 cups water
  2 tablespoons (¼ stick) butter
  1¼ cups cornmeal
  ¼ cup Parmesan cheese
  Salt and pepper to taste
  2 tablespoons oil

1 clove garlic, chopped
3 large basil leaves, chiffonade
1 small Roma tomato, diced
  (optional)
¼ cup red wine
¼ cup demi-glace *or* beef or chicken
  stock
½ cup (1 stick) butter

Wild Mushroom Ragout
  2 tablespoons olive oil
  1 pound wild mushrooms, such as
    oyster, chanterelle, shiitake, morel,
    and button

Poached Eggs
  6–8 eggs
  ¼ cup hollandaise or crème fraîche

1. *For the polenta:* Bring the liquid and butter to a gentle boil; reduce the heat. Gradually add the cornmeal and Parmesan while whisking. Add salt and pepper and continue stirring with a wooden spoon until the mixture is thick enough for spoon to stand.

2. Transfer the polenta onto a greased baking sheet. Use a spatula to flatten it to ¼-inch thickness. Refrigerate until firm, approximately 20 minutes. Once polenta is firm, cut into 2-inch squares or rounds and sauté in hot oil until golden on both sides.

3. *For the mushroom ragout:* Heat the olive oil in a large skillet. Add the fresh mushrooms, garlic, basil, and diced tomatoes. Sauté until the mushrooms start to lightly brown on the edges. Add the red wine and demi-glace and simmer until the mixture's volume is reduced by two-thirds. Whisk in the cold butter.

4. Poach or fry the eggs.

5. Spoon the Wild Mushroom Ragout onto plates with polenta rounds. Top with a poached or fried egg and dollop with hollandaise or crème fraîche.

Serves 6–8

Café au Lait and Beignets

Café au Lait and Beignets

1 tablespoon active dry yeast

1½ cups warm water (approximately 105 degrees)

¾ cup granulated sugar

1 teaspoon salt

3 eggs, beaten

½ cup buttermilk

1 cup evaporated milk

6–7 cups all-purpose flour

¼ cup shortening

Oil, for deep frying

Powdered sugar

Coffee

1. In a large bowl, sprinkle the yeast over the warm water; stir to dissolve and let stand for 5 minutes. Add the sugar, salt, beaten eggs, buttermilk, and evaporated milk. Whisk to blend thoroughly.

2. Add 4 cups of the flour; beat until smooth. Add the shortening; gradually blend in the remaining flour. Cover with plastic wrap and chill for at least 4 hours or overnight.

3. Remove the dough from the refrigerator and roll it out on a floured board to ⅛-inch thickness. Cut into 2½- to 3-inch squares. Let these rise for approximately 20 minutes.

4. In a deep fryer, heat oil 2 inches deep to 360 degrees.

5. Deep-fry the beignets for 2 to 3 minutes until lightly browned on both sides. Drain on paper towels and sprinkle generously with powdered sugar. Serve hot with coffee.

Chef's Note: The dough can be cut and frozen and allowed to rise again before frying.

Serves 6–8

Bread Pudding French Toast
with Caramelized Banana Syrup

Bread Pudding
  2 cups whole milk
  1 cup heavy cream
  1/3 cup packed dark brown sugar
  7 large eggs
  1 teaspoon pure vanilla extract
  12 slices bread (sourdough or French
    works best)
  2 tablespoons (1/4 stick) unsalted
    butter, at room temperature

1 teaspoon ground cinnamon

Caramelized Banana Syrup
  1/4 cup (1/2 stick) butter
  1 cup packed brown sugar
  1/2 teaspoon ground cinnamon
  4 bananas, cut in half lengthwise,
    then halved

1. *For the bread pudding:* In a medium sauce pot, bring the milk and cream just to a boil. Remove from the heat and whisk in the sugar. Allow the milk to cool for 15 minutes.

2. In a large bowl, whisk together the eggs and vanilla. Add the milk mixture and whisk well.

3. Butter a bread pan or deep baking dish. Tear the bread into large chunks, sprinkle with cinnamon, and slowly pour the egg–milk mixture over the bread. You may have to stop every once in a while to allow the liquid to seep in. Once you've poured it all in, press down on the bread with your fingers to submerge it. Cover the dish and refrigerate for at least an hour, or even overnight.

4. Preheat the oven to 350 degrees.

5. Bake the French toast for an hour or until a knife inserted in the center comes out clean. When the bread pudding cools, remove it from the pan and cut it into slices approximately 1/2-inch thick. When you're almost ready to serve, lightly butter a skillet and sauté each slice.

6. *For the banana syrup:* Place the butter, sugar, and cinnamon in a noncorrosive saucepan or skillet. Let the mixture melt by whisking the butter and sugar together over medium heat. Once it starts to thicken and caramelize, reduce the heat to low, add the bananas, turn the heat to high for 1 minute, and then turn it off. Spoon over the French toast. Top with whipped cream.

Serves 6–8

Bread Pudding French Toast with Caramelized Banana Syrup

Michael Merilli and Adobe Grand Villas

Grilled Duck Breast with Armagnac and Figs

6-8 duck breast fillets
1 cup molasses
1 cup white wine
¼ cup demi-glace or beef stock
6 ounces fig preserves

6 dried figs, sliced
¼ teaspoon raspberry vinegar
2 tablespoons Armagnac (French-style cognac)

1. Heat a gas or charcoal grill.

2. Wash and pat dry the duck breasts, score a few crosses in the fat side with a sharp knife, and marinate in molasses for 20 to 30 minutes. Rinse the breasts off and pat them dry again. Place the breasts skin-side down on the hot grill until the skin is almost black from char, 10 to 15 minutes. Turn the breast over and continue grilling for about 5 minutes. Let the duck rest for a few minutes before slicing.

3. In a saucepan over moderate heat, add the white wine and stock; simmer this mixture for 5 minutes. Add the fig preserves and dried figs and continue simmering until it's reduced by half. Finish by adding the raspberry vinegar and Armagnac.

4. Slice the duck breasts to about ⅛-inch thickness and fan them out on the plate, topping with sauce.

Serves 6–8

Grilled Duck Breast with Armagnac and Figs

12

Ivan Flowers
and the Gallery on Oak Creek

Ivan Flowers's long list of accolades and the prestigious restaurants that have made up his career, including most recently the Four Diamond Gallery on Oak Creek at Amara Resort and Spa, all started with his father. Ivan's dad was the chef and owner of Rendezvous Restaurant in New York, and Ivan says his earliest memory is of standing beside a huge pot and cooking with his dad. He can still taste his dad's turkey barley soup . . . but to this day has been unable to replicate it. "My father would say, 'To be a chef it must be in your blood to be in your heart.' We all must cook with heart. Your inspiration, the places you've been, the time of day, your emotions and spirit and passion can all be tasted in the food you cook."

Ivan grew up in Brooklyn and initially pursued a career in psychology and social work—he has a bachelor's degree in psychology from the New York Institute of Technology—before realizing he was destined to follow in his father's footsteps. He went to work for a restaurant in Washington state before deciding to head to warmer climes and attend the Scottsdale Culinary Institute; he graduated with a degree in culinary arts and restaurant management in 1997. He went on to work for some of the most sophisticated restaurants in Arizona, including T. Cooks at Scottsdale's Royal Palms Resort, Mary Elaine's at the Phoenician, and Different Point of View at Pointe Hilton Tapatio Cliffs Resort in Phoenix. He also returned to the Scottsdale Culinary Institute to act as the lead instructor and chef at L'Ecole restaurant. During this time the restaurant had a three-month waiting list and received its highest Zagat Survey rating. In November 2007 Ivan made the move to Sedona and the Gallery on Oak Creek.

Ivan Flowers, executive chef of the Gallery on Oak Creek

Ivan redesigned the Gallery from the decor and the dishes to the breakfast, lunch, and dinner menus. Gone is the artwork that previously adorned each table and gave the restaurant its name: "Now the food is the art," says Ivan. Floor-to-ceiling windows offer views of the red rocks and the lush foliage surrounding Oak Creek, located just steps from the restaurant. During the warmer months it's a treat to grab a bottle of wine and sit on the patio. Inside, silver chain maille covers the windows that separate the restaurant from the hotel's lobby, the linens are a crisp cream and black, and the white china plates are absolutely enormous. For special occasions, make reservations to dine in the Gallery's wine room surrounded by 2,000 bottles of wine from nearly 250 labels (the Gallery on Oak Creek has won *Wine Spectator*'s Best of Award of Excellence four years in a row). Ivan brought eight people with him to the Gallery—"the chef and his posse," jokes Michael Rock, Amara's general manager—and continues to base his kitchen on developing new chefs.

"It's an eclectic kitchen," says the goateed Ivan. "We're a think tank, a lab for young chefs. We have revelations once a day. We're a completely different kitchen—there are no egos, we all learn from each other."

The Gallery on Oak Creek dining room

Ivan calls the cuisine at the Gallery "global fusion." He brought with him a few signature dishes but plans on changing the menu three times a year. Popular small plates and soups include the Pan-Seared La Belle Farms Foie Gras with Preserved Citrus Onion Marmalade, Truffle-Scented Beignets and Extra Vecchio Drizzle, as well as the Black Trumpet Mushroom Infused Lobster Bisque—one of the thickest, most flavorful soups you'll ever taste. Ivan says his Rack of Lamb with Garlic Basil Persillade, Creamy Belgian Salsify, and Thyme-Scented Baby Artichokes is one of his most popular large-plate items, while for dessert he's received rave reviews for his Blue Cheese Ice Cream. Seafood is flown in fresh daily, and Ivan balances local ingredients—he's currently building a chef's garden in Sedona where he can grow his own produce—with global items such as mangoes from Chile, cheeses from Vermont, and mushrooms from the Pacific, Southwest, and Italy.

But perhaps Ivan's most unusual offering is his tasting menu. Once a table requests a tasting menu, Ivan meets with everyone to choose a theme—vegetarian, lactose-free, shellfish, what have you. None of the items comes from the regular menu—Ivan creates everything off the top of his head, on the spot. Even if several tables request the same theme, none of the items will be the same. Ivan's record: thirty-six tasting menus in one night. Not too surprising from a chef who says he doesn't like recipes, but it amazes Michael all the same.

"It's incredible," he says with a shake of his head. "Since Ivan came on board, we've heard from guests who've said it was the finest meal they've ever had, with food they've never seen before."

Amara—the name combines the words *amore* and *terra*, or "love of the land"—opened in 2004 with a hundred boutique rooms, thirty-two of which have whirlpool bathtubs and twenty-four with patios overlooking Oak Creek. *Condé Nast Traveler* readers named the property one of the 721 best places to stay in the world in 2008. Resort amenities include star and spa parties, yoga classes, wine tastings, valet parking, and DVD rentals. Amara is the only spa in Arizona to feature Elemis products, a London-based line of body and skin care potions. For those looking to lounge a little longer in the spa's East-meets-West-themed relaxation room, Ivan has a special spa menu with items such as Thin-Sliced French Limousine Style Roast Beef and Balsamic Lemon Glazed Watermelon Cubes—and the food can be delivered directly to you at the spa. The Gallery also offers a spa continental breakfast.

Chef Flowers's Tricks of the Trade

"Cook things you love to eat yourself—be a minimalist and respect the product. Keep an open mind. Use your fingers when seasoning—feel the spices leave your fingers, and your body will tell you when you've added enough. Flavor dictates plating, so consider the taste and mouth-feel first; when everything is delicious, plating comes naturally. You'll be in trouble if you think about plating before making the meal delicious. Balance your salts and sweets. There should be a gentleness to the food—it shouldn't be too salty or lack seasoning."

At Home

Chef Flowers doesn't cook much at home and admits he eats out often. "I like to be in an industrial kitchen, and I don't like to cook on my time away—I want to be able to come into the kitchen fresh every day. I'll make myself the occasional tuna fish sandwich or Chinese food. My tastes are simple. I can get turned on by a turkey Reuben as much as by foie gras. Good food doesn't need to be expensive. You can do magic to peanut butter and jelly."

Gallery on Oak Creek at Amara Resort and Spa
310 North Highway 89A, Sedona
928-282-4828
www.amararesort.com

Fruit Trilogy: Spiced Jalapeño Meyer Lemon Drizzle

2 Meyer lemons
Pinch of Fleur de Sel (sea salt)
¼ teaspoon sugar
⅛ teaspoon Champagne vinegar
1 jalapeño pepper

6 pieces seedless watermelon, cut 5x3
  inches
6 pieces honeydew, cut 5x3 inches
6 pieces cantaloupe, cut 5x3 inches

1. Juice the lemons and place them in a small saucepan. Bring to a quick boil, turn off the heat, and add the salt, sugar, vinegar, and split jalapeño. Let the glaze stand at room temperature for 1 hour.

2. Brush your chilled fruit pieces with the glaze. Arrange the fruit on plates.

Serves 6

Fruit Trilogy: Spiced Jalapeño Meyer Lemon Drizzle

Deconstructed Salad Niçoise

Ahi
  Pinch of coriander powder
  Salt and pepper to taste
  1 pound center-cut Hawaiian
    sashimi-grade-one ahi tuna
  1 teaspoon olive oil

Potatoes
  2 cups duck fat
  3 cloves garlic
  6 whole black peppercorns
  6 fingerling potatoes
  Salt and pepper to taste

Truffle Egg Mousse
  4 hard-boiled duck eggs
  ¼ cup porcini oil
  ¼ teaspoon black truffle oil
  3 caperberries (brined), split in half,
    for garnish

Haricots Verts
  ¾ pound *haricots verts*
  6 sheets gelatin

Olive Tapenade
  1 cup mixed Provençal olives, pitted
  Pinch of porcini oil (about 3 drops)

1. *For the ahi:* Sprinkle salt, pepper, and coriander on the ahi. Sear each side in a hot sauté pan with the olive oil for 20 seconds. Refrigerate.

2. *For the potatoes:* Cut the fingerlings into ¼-inch slices. Heat the duck fat with the garlic and peppercorns to a light rolling boil. Place the potatoes in the fat and simmer till al dente, about 15 minutes. Remove the pan from the heat; drain the potatoes, place them in a bowl, season with salt and pepper, and reserve.

3. *For the Truffle Egg Mousse:* Place the eggs, porcini oil, and truffle oil in the blender and puree. Season with salt and pepper. When the mixture is cool, shape into six quenelles (oval dumplings).

4. *For the* haricots verts: Boil the *haricots verts* till they're al dente, then plunge them into cold water. Take a third of the green beans and blend in a food processor with ⅛ cup of the water they cooled in. Strain the liquid through a chinois or fine-mesh strainer and refrigerate for 4 hours.

5. Bloom six sheets of gelatin into the chilled *haricot vert* juice. Place the remainder of *haricots verts* into a terrine mold and cover with the gelatin juice mixture. Refrigerate for 3 hours.

Deconstructed Salad Niçoise

6. *For the olive tapenade:* Blend the pitted olives with the porcini oil in a food processor till smooth. Reserve.

7. *Assembly:* Cut the ahi into twenty-four thin slices. Cut the *haricot vert* mold into ¼-inch slices. Set out six square serving plates.

8. Onto the center of each plate, spoon some olive tapenade, then spread it out by raking it with the tines of a fork. Put four slices of ahi on top. Place some potatoes in one corner of the plate and an egg mousse quenelle in another corner topped with a split caperberrry. Arrange a slice of *haricots verts* in a third corner and serve.

Serves 6

Milk-Fed Rack of Lamb with Garlic Basil Persillade, Creamy Belgian Salsify, and Thyme-Scented Baby Artichokes

Herb Butter

1 pound unsalted butter, softened (preferably Plugrá, a butterfat-rich version sold in specialty markets)

2 tablespoons minced fresh garlic

2 tablespoons chopped fresh basil

Salt and pepper to taste

Lamb Rack

3 26-ounce Frenched racks of lamb

6 pieces 3-inch-cut domestic lamb shank

Salt and pepper to taste

2 tablespoons Italian lemon olive oil

1 cup panko (Japanese bread crumbs)

Salsify

1 pound Belgian salsify

1 quart milk

4 cups reduced heavy cream (12 cups reduced to 4 cups over low heat)

Salt and pepper to taste

Artichokes

1 pound baby artichokes

Olive oil, for sautéing

1 tablespoon garlic puree

½ cup white wine

2 sprigs fresh thyme

1. *For the herb butter:* Combine the softened butter with the garlic, basil, and salt and pepper to taste. Roll the butter into a tubular shape with parchment paper and refrigerate for 2 hours.

2. *For the lamb rack:* Preheat the oven to 450 degrees. Salt and pepper the lamb. Place all of the pieces in a medium-hot ovenproof sauté pan with the oil and sear until the meat is caramelized on the fat side. Turn the meat over and place the pan into the oven for 5 minutes.

3. Remove the pan from the oven and sprinkle bread crumbs on the lamb. Place four medallions of herb butter on top, then sprinkle more bread crumbs on the butter. Reserve.

4. *For the salsify:* Peel the salsify, cut it into 2-inch pieces, and place it in the cold milk. Bring to a simmer and cook until al dente, about 30 minutes. Add the reduced cream and cook for 5 minutes more, season with salt and pepper, and reserve.

5. *For the artichokes:* Peel the baby artichokes and cut in half. Sauté for 6 minutes in olive oil. Add the garlic puree and continue cooking until a fond develops on the bottom of the pan. Deglaze with the white wine, add the thyme, and cover with parchment paper. Steam-sauté the artichokes over low heat for 15 minutes or until al dente. Reserve.

Chef's Note: The term *fond* refers to the caramelized, concentrated brown bits and pieces of meat—or in this case vegetables—left behind in the pan after sautéing. This leftover is used to make flavorful sauces and stocks.

6. *Assembly:* Return the lamb to the 450-degree oven and cook for 8 to 9 minutes, then remove from the oven and let it rest for 4 minutes. Place the heated salsify and artichokes in the middle of the plate. Cut three chops and arrange on top with a piece of lamb shank.

Serves 6

Milk-Fed Rack of Lamb with Garlic Basil
Persillade, Creamy Belgian Salsify, and
Thyme-Scented Baby Artichokes

Seared Foie Gras, Maui Onion Marmalade, Herb Peppadew Sauce, and Extra Vecchio Balsamico Drizzle

Marmalade
1 teaspoon Italian lemon olive oil
1 large Maui onion
¼ cup aged port
1 tablespoon aged balsamic vinegar
1 teaspoon Vinagres de Yema
   (50-year-old sherry vinegar)
¼ cup Cointreau orange liqueur
¼ teaspoon finely chopped fresh
   herbs (a combination of thyme,
   oregano, chives, and tarragon)
Pinch of sel gris (sea salt)
Pepper to taste

Peppadew Sauce
5 small South African piquante peppadew peppers (pickled)

1 tablespoon unsalted butter
   (preferably Plugrá, a butterfat-rich
   version sold in specialty markets)
Pinch of sel gris
Pepper to taste

Foie Gras
6 3-ounce pieces foie gras (about ⅓
   cup per piece) (La Belle Farms or
   Hudson Valley recommended)
Pinch of sel gris
Fresh-cracked black pepper to taste
Extra vecchio balsamico (aged balsamic vinegar) (balsamic vinegar
   can be substituted, but reduce by
   one-third over low heat before
   using)

1. *For the marmalade:* Place the lemon oil in a small saucepan over medium heat. Julienne the onion, add to the oil, and cook until translucent. Add the aged port, aged vinegars, and orange liqueur; cook over a low flame until the mixture is syrupy, about 20 minutes. Add the fresh herbs and season with salt and pepper. Set the marmalade aside at room temperature.

2. *For the peppadew sauce:* Place the peppadews in a food processor and blend until smooth. Add the butter. Season with salt and pepper. Set aside at room temperature.

3. *For the foie gras:* Preheat the oven to 450 degrees. Season the foie gras with sel gris and pepper. Sear it in an ovenproof sauté pan over high heat for 45 seconds. Turn the foie over and place the pan in the oven for 3 minutes.

Seared Foie Gras, Maui Onion Marmalade, Herb Peppadew Sauce, and Extra Vecchio Balsamico Drizzle

4. *Assembly:* Place a small amount of marmalade on each plate. Surround with peppadew sauce and place a piece of foie gras on top. Drizzle extra vecchio balsamico on the foie gras.

Serves 6

Poached Maine Lobster with Seared Diver Scallops, Truffled Petite Brussels Sprouts, and Herbed Lobster Butter

Lobsters
- 6 very lively Maine lobsters, 1 pound each
- 6 quarts court bouillon
- 1 cup Chardonnay
- 1 pound unsalted butter (preferably Plugrá, a butterfat-rich version sold in specialty markets)
- Salt and pepper to taste

Herbed Lobster Butter
- 2 onions, diced
- 2 carrots, diced
- 2 fennel bulbs, diced
- 1 stalk celery, diced
- 10 cloves garlic, peeled
- 2 tablespoons tomato paste
- 2 cups brandy
- 2 cups port
- 2 cups vermouth
- 3 quarts fresh chicken stock
- Sprig of fresh thyme
- 2 ounces dried porcini mushrooms
- 1 pound unsalted butter (preferably Plugrá)
- Salt and pepper to taste
- 1/4 teaspoon chopped fresh tarragon

Brussels Sprouts
- 1 pound petite brussels sprouts, trimmed and cut in half
- Olive oil
- 3 droplets black truffle oil
- Salt and pepper to taste
- Butter

Scallops
- Salt and pepper to taste
- 12 U-8 dry-pack diver scallops
- 1 teaspoon Italian lemon olive oil
- Sprig of fresh thyme
- Butter

1. *For the lobsters:* Remove the claws, tails, and all viscera from each lobster; reserve the head. Bring the court bouillon to a boil and boil the claws for 5 minutes, then plunge them into ice water. Return the bouillon to a boil and place in the tails for 4 minutes, then plunge them into ice water. After the lobsters are cold (about 10 minutes), remove them from their shells. Split the tails and remove all cartilage from the claws with tweezers.

2. In a saucepan, reduce the Chardonnay by half, then whisk in the butter. Add salt and pepper to taste. Place the lobsters in this butter mixture and poach for 4 minutes.

Poached Maine Lobster with Seared Diver Scallops, Truffled Petite Brussels Sprouts, and Herbed Lobster Butter

3. *For the Herbed Lobster Butter:* Place the lobster bodies into a large, hot sauce pot with a little oil and sauté until they're bright red. Add the vegetables and garlic cloves and cook until the onions are translucent. Add the tomato paste and cook until a fond forms on the bottom of the pot. Deglaze with the brandy and cook until the mixture reaches a syrup consistency. Add the port and again, cook to a syrup consistency. Add the vermouth and cook to a syrup (au sec). Cover with the chicken stock; add the thyme. Simmer for 45 minutes and strain through a fine-mesh strainer.

4. Pour the strained mixture into a new sauce pot. Add the porcini mushrooms and reduce the stock by seven-eighths or to a thick glaze. Measure out 2 cups of this glaze (reserve the rest in the refrigerator for other uses) and whisk in the butter in increments; don't allow the mixture to get too hot. Season to taste with salt and pepper; add the chopped tarragon. The finished butter sauce should be kept warm until serving.

5. *For the brussels sprouts:* Plunge the halved sprouts into boiling water for 20 seconds, then plunge them into ice water. Over medium heat, sauté the blanched brussels sprouts in a little olive oil with the truffle oil for 2 minutes, then add salt and pepper to taste. Finish by adding a little butter to glaze. Keep warm.

6. *For the scallops:* Salt and pepper the scallops in a hot sauté pan with the lemon oil, caramelize one side, turn over, add the thyme and a pat of butter, then baste. Put the pan in a 450-degree oven for 3 minutes.

7. *Assembly:* On each plate, arrange some of the poached lobster meat, along with two scallops. Put brussels sprouts in the middle, then drizzle Herbed Lobster Butter over the seafood.

Serves 6

Metric Conversion Tables

Approximate U.S.–Metric Equivalents

Liquid Ingredients		Dry Ingredients		
U.S. Measures	Metric	U.S. Measures		Metric
¼ tsp.	1.23 ml	17³/₅ oz.	1 livre	500 g
½ tsp.	2.36 ml	16 oz.	1 lb.	454 g
¾ tsp.	3.70 ml	8⁷/₈ oz.		250 g
1 tsp.	4.93 ml	5¼ oz.		150 g
1¼ tsp.	6.16 ml	4½ oz.		125 g
1½ tsp.	7.39 ml	4 oz.		115 (113.2) g
1³/₄ tsp.	8.63 ml	3½ oz.		100 g
2 tsp.	9.86 ml	3 oz.		85 (84.9) g
1 Tbsp.	14.79 ml	2⁴/₅ oz.		80 g
2 Tbsp.	29.57 ml	2 oz.		60 (56.6) g
3 Tbsp.	44.36 ml	1³/₄ oz.		50 g
¼ cup	59.15 ml	1 oz.		30 (28.3) g
½ cup	118.30 ml	⁷/₈ oz.		25 g
1 cup	236.59 ml	¾ oz.		21 (21.3) g
2 cups or 1 pt.	473.18 ml	½ oz.		15 (14.2) g
3 cups	709.77 ml	¼ oz.		7 (7.1) g
4 cups or 1 qt.	946.36 ml	⅛ oz.		3½ (3.5) g
4 qts. or 1 gal.	3.79 lt	¹/₁₆ oz.		2 (1.8) g

Recipe Index

Index